OVERCOMING
TIME POVERTY

How to Achieve More By Working Less

Bill Quain, Ph.D.

Overcoming Time Poverty
Bill Quain, Ph.D.

Published by Wales Publishing Company
Miami Beach, Florida
Wales Publishing Company is exclusively owned and operated by Bill Quain
www.quain.com

Cover design by Parry Design – *parrydesign.com*

Printed in the United States of America
First printing – September 2005
ISBN: 0-9623646-4-9
Library of Congress Control Number: 2005907557

distributed by Executive Books.com

Table of Contents

Acknowledgements

This book was a real family effort. My wife, Jeanne Quain, was much more than an editor. She patiently listened to my theories, subtly influenced my thoughts, edited each chapter numerous times and, in the end, was a real partner in my book.

My daughters Amanda and Kathleen Quain were remarkable — editing and proofreading the manuscript on their laptops, and even reading it out loud on long car trips. Thanks girls!

My dad, Bill Quain Sr., was a constant source of encouragement and information. He sent me a steady stream of articles clipped from newspapers and magazines. And, he was one of the final readers. His comments on content and context made this a better book.

My mother-in-law, Janet Wockenfuss, did a remarkable job on the final manuscript. Her page-by-page comments alerted us to several problems and her suggestions created some great phrases.

Finally, a special thanks to professional editor Mark Hayes. Mark stepped in when the manuscript was just a collection of random chapters. He was always willing to do the work until it was right. Great job, Mark.

Dedication

In memory of Kay D. Quain.
A great author, publisher and a wonderful Mother.
Thanks Mom.

Introduction

The difference between time and money is this: You know when you're out of money.

—Bill Quain

Why Are You Reading This Book?

You're probably reading this book because you think you don't have enough time in your life. And you probably think you can fix this problem if you can just become more efficient.

If that's the way you feel, then close this book, take it back to the store, and get a refund. I can't help you. You see, this is *not* a book about becoming more efficient *at what you are doing now*. There are books on time management to help organize your life. Go get one of them.

The truth is, you are already efficient at what you are doing! You don't need more time to do the same things you are doing now. *You need to do **different things** in order to have **more** time in your life!*

If you are a typical person reading this

If you are like most people, you are:

- **Working an average of 49 hours per week at your job—or more!**
- **Part of a two-income family.**
- **Putting your kids in day care so you have more time to earn money.**
- **In credit card debt.**
- **Refinancing your home mortgage to pay off debts or tuition. Or both.**
- **40% more efficient and productive than you were five years ago.**
- **Trying to earn more money by getting a promotion or raise at work.**
- **Scheduling your children for after-school activities at least three days per week.**
- **Doing a job that it took one-and-a-half people to do five years ago.**
- **Wondering what happened to your time!**

---

book, you sense you are in trouble. You have overscheduled your life and the lives of your children. You can't seem to get ahead. You can't even seem to keep up. You reach the end of each day completely exhausted, stressed out, and dreading another day, another month, another year of this frenzied existence.

Yet, you are part of the most productive, most efficient workforce that ever inhabited this planet. You have technology at your fingertips, convenience foods to prepare, entertainment in your living room, and 24-hour access to the world via the World Wide Web.

You are doing everything at the speed of light. You have voice-mail, e-mail, instant messaging and downloadable movies. You don't have to wait for anything.

And you thought I would teach you how to do all this stuff faster? No way.

Not Time Management? Then What Is This Book About?

I am going to teach you to overcome *Time Poverty*. I define *Time Poverty* like this:

> **When you don't have the time to do the things you really WANT to do, because you are too busy doing the things you think you HAVE to do.**

Let me repeat that, so it really sinks in:

> **Time Poverty is: When you don't have the time to do the things you really WANT to do, because you are too busy doing the things you think you HAVE to do.**

When we think of poverty, we usually think in terms of financial poverty. But unlike financially poor people who don't have money, Time-Poor people *do* have time. Remember, everyone gets the same 24 hours each day.

You *will* learn to overcome Time Poverty in this book. I will teach you a simple 5-step system to get out of this rat race by getting off the Fast Track at work. You will learn how to reconnect with the important people in your life. You will learn to live fully, and teach other people to do the same.

Two Concepts to Remember as You Read This Book: LifeTimers and Time Equity

I was recently talking to my daughter. "I am having trouble coming up with a good word to describe people's lifetime for my book," I told her. "I want to show readers how their time is always running. They need to use it, or lose it!"

"I am reading a book that has something like that in it," she said. "They have a big hourglass with no bottom on it. It's called a LifeTimer."

Wow! That was the clue I needed. And, it explained why so many people are living in Time Poverty. They think their lives are like an hourglass, rather than like a LifeTimer.

Look at the two pictures below. One of them, the traditional hourglass, is how most people measure their time. They spend their time by the hour. They go to work and trade their time: an hour's work for an hour's pay.

But your LifeTimer is different. Unlike an hourglass, when the sands of time run through your LifeTimer, that sand is gone forever. You can't turn the glass over. And, unlike the hourglass, you don't know how much time you have in your LifeTimer.

Hourglass   *LifeTimer*

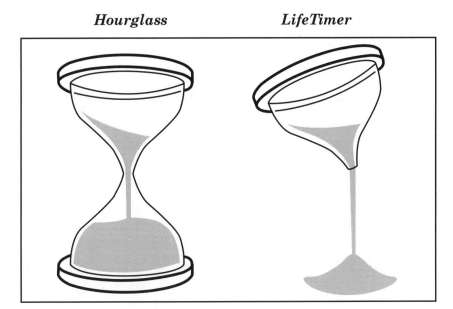

Time-Rich people know they have a LifeTimer. They use their time as it runs out of the glass. They can't save it. They can't get any more of it. They need to use it minute-by-minute.

If you spend your time working for money, you can't use your time for anything else. However, if you put your money to work *for* you, you can use your time for whatever you want! As you'll see, that is one of the secrets to overcoming Time Poverty.

Time Equity

In order to overcome Time Poverty, you have to understand another simple, but very powerful concept called Time Equity. *Equity* is something you own. We will discuss different types of equity in this book. You can create equity, or it can be given to you. In either case, it is yours.

Time Equity is the *total* of all the time you own. We all own time, from the moment we are born. It doesn't matter if you are born wealthy or poor. You own your time.

Throughout this book, you'll hear me say you should not trade your Time Equity for dollars, but use your Time Equity to create other kinds of equity. You can then let *that* equity create dollars! You see folks, it isn't just *time* that's running out of your LifeTimer, it's Time Equity. Save more time for your life, and spend less time on your work. If you trade something besides time for dollars, you have more dollars *and* more time!

What's Next?

Overcoming Time Poverty is divided into two parts, **Time Games** and **How to Create a Time-Rich Life**. You'll find a brief summary at the beginning of each section.

Speaking of the beginning, are you ready to get started? Time's up! Let's go!

Part 1

Time Games

Part 1

Time Games

I brought my boat to the shop the other day. The motors were not running properly. I asked the repair man what it would take to make the motors work the way they were supposed to.

"Before I can tell you what we need to do to make the engines run smoothly, I need to find out what's wrong with them," he said. "Then, I need to see how they got into this condition, so it won't happen again."

That's what Part 1, **Time Games**, is all about. First, I am going to help you discover what's wrong—why you seem to have no time in your life. Then, we will look at what *caused* your situation.

In **Time Games** you will learn why you are out of time. It isn't because you are overscheduled, or inefficient. It isn't because your boss is inflexible, or the pace of life has gotten too fast. Sure, all those things make it a little hectic. The real problem is that you are playing the *wrong game*!

What do I mean by that? Here's an example. You probably think your life is supposed to be "played" by trading your time for money at a job, or in a small business. The problem is, in *that* game, work takes up too much of your time! It doesn't leave enough time for the really good things in life.

You need to play a game you can win, a game where the rules work to your advantage. But, you can't start doing that until you understand what the wrong games are. Reading **Time Games** is your first step towards understanding how you got into this situation to begin with. It's your first step to overcome Time Poverty.

Don't worry though, Part 2, **How to Create a Time-Rich Life**, will show you how to *fix* the problem—for good. But, just like my boat mechanic, you need to understand what's going wrong before you can make it right.

Chapter 1

You Have to Play the Right Game

If life doesn't offer a game worth playing, then invent a new one.

— Anthony J. D'Angelo

Play the Right Game

Last month, 11 workers in a dental office won $15 Million dollars, and they were playing the wrong game—or so they thought. The 11 co-workers from Ohio had been pooling their money for about a year, playing the multi-state, mega lottery game. On this particular week, however, they gave the money to someone who had never purchased the tickets before. Instead of buying the multi-state game tickets, the worker played the money on the Ohio state lottery.

The six numbers matched! They won $15 million dollars!

The headlines read, "Lottery winners played wrong game." But, did they? NO! As it turned out, they played exactly the right game. If they had played the wrong game, they wouldn't have won. Ten of those people wanted to play the wrong game, but luckily, the one who bought the tickets played the right game.

Life is like that. Most people are playing the wrong game. They can't possibly win. But, every now and then, someone comes along and does it right. Sometimes, it is just dumb luck— like the Ohio Lottery winners. Sometimes, however, you are shown an example. Sometimes, something happens that makes it all perfectly clear.

It Happened To Me!

If you read my book, *10 Rules To Break & 10 Rules To Make*, then you already know what happened to me. On July 7, 1993, at 2:30 in the afternoon, my life changed forever.

My wife, Jeanne, and I were sitting at a dockside restaurant next to the Intracoastal Waterway in Fort Lauderdale, Florida. Jeanne was pregnant with our second daughter Kathleen, while Amanda, age 2, was sleeping in a stroller. We were living in Orlando, but I had just given a talk at a hotel on the beach in Fort Lauderdale.

It was a hot day. Sitting next to the waterway, Jeanne and I were talking about our most pressing disappointment. We wanted to live on the water. It was our dream, our passion. But, we just didn't have the money to do it. And, I couldn't seem to find the time to get the money!

Suddenly, a shadow fell across our table. I looked up to see a large, private yacht cruising slowly down the waterway. On the stern was a group of happy people. They were drinking champagne and laughing. They were having a great time. In fact, they were doing exactly what *I* wanted to do—having fun on the water!

Folks, that was the moment it hit me. July 7, 1993, at 2:30 in the afternoon. Up till that point, I had always thought that the people who lived like that were different than me. But, for whatever reason, on that day, at that moment, I had a massive, life changing revelation.

Those people were not different from me. In fact, they were exactly like me. They just ACTED different than I did. They had what they wanted because they were playing a different game. They were playing the right game. And, if I wanted what they had, all I had to do was play the right game too!

I didn't have the things I wanted—living on the water, a nice boat, and time to enjoy myself—because the game I was playing just didn't go there. Even if I won my game, it wouldn't give me that kind of lifestyle. No matter how well, or how hard, or how long you play the wrong game, it will never give you the results you want. You have to play the right game to get the right results.

What Are The Right Results?

Everyone has a different dream for their lives. You may want to live on the water, like we did. You might want something else. Maybe your dream is to build a hospital, or travel on long vacations. But folks, no matter what your dream is, you need two things: time and money. In this book, you will learn how to have both! You will learn how to create wealth—without spending all your time doing it.

Most people are clueless when it comes to getting time *and* money. They know how to make money. They go to work and trade their time for it. This will get you money, but not time. And, most people know how to get more time. They cut back on work. This gets you time, but no money. Both systems cause a lot of stress. You are either out of time or money, and you lose sleep worrying about the one you don't have.

You want time AND money. The only way to get those results is to play the right game. You have to make changes in your life. Think different, act different, play different, and you can have different results. Play the game that time and money rich people play, and you can get what they have.

The "Work and Hope" Game

The vast majority of people play the "Work and Hope" Game. They get a job, plan to work for forty or fifty years, and then hope that something comes along to get them out of that work! That is why they play the lottery. They know that they will never have the time to enjoy life unless they get a sudden windfall.

They hope that something big will happen, because they know that what they are doing will never give them time and money. No one they work with has time and money. Their families don't have it, and their friends don't have it. They work and hope, work and hope.

They are playing the wrong game.

What About That Lottery?

In Florida, where I live, the lottery jackpot starts at about $6 million dollars. If you win the $6 million, you can take it all in one lump sum or you can receive about $200,000 per year for the next 20 years. In either case, you will suddenly have more choices than you do now!

Lottery winners win money, but much more importantly, *they win time*! If you have money, and if you get that money in a way that doesn't require you to give up all your time, you can choose to use that money in your *own* time.

What would you do with an extra $200,000 per year *in take-home pay*? It certainly would make life easier. You could afford to hire people to do the things you don't like to do. You wouldn't have to take overtime work or an extra job to save up for college tuition for your kids. You wouldn't have to take out a loan for your next car. Money may not buy happiness, but it does give you power and freedom.

Making Money versus Winning Money

You may HOPE you win the lottery, but, the chances are, you won't! So, what if you had to *earn* that money the way you do now? What if they gave you a $200,000 raise each year? How much extra work would you have to do on your job to make an additional $200,000 each year?

If you need more money in order to have more time in your life, and if you have to *earn* that money, and if earning that money is going to take up so much time that you will have even *less* time at the end of each day, *then you have to get that money some other way than earning it on a job.*

How About Playing a New Game?

Let's play a different game, one you can win! In this game, you can:

1. Have a job that you really enjoy—because you will be doing things you like without worrying about the next raise or the next promotion. And, you can relax and do things you like *away* from work.

2. Create a great second income—on your own time! You will learn how to have fun and make money. You won't be trading your time for dollars, you will be creating wealth.

3. Multiply that money into *equity*. Equity will generate even

more money—giving you even more time and choices.

Along the way, you will learn one of the most important tools you have ever come across—how to increase the *value* of each and every hour of your life. You will learn how to create a Time-Rich, relationship-rich, ego-rich, fulfilling lifestyle. You will discover the meaning of the new retirement, a retirement that can come at any age.

Does that sound like a better game than the one you are playing now? Isn't it better to do something positive than to HOPE that something will happen?

Five Rules for a New Game

Every game has rules. Every game has strategies to follow to win the grand prize. Here are five things you

Time Out – Do You Want to Sleep Less or Work Less?

You bought this book to get more time. Fair enough. But where will that time come from? There are only 24 hours in the day. You can't create more time, so if you want more time to do the things you like to do, you need to take that time from some other place.

Where do we spend our time? It is almost equally divided into three parts: sleep, work, and everything else! That's right. One third of our time is devoted to sleeping or at least trying to get to sleep. Another third is spent working, or getting ready for work, or commuting to and from work. That leaves only one third of our time for everything else, including recreation, cooking, cleaning, taking care of the family, building relationships, walking the dog, running errands, and so forth.

Where am I supposed to find the time you want me to give you? I hope you don't want me to cut out some of your personal time! You already have only a few short hours to get everything done. The only other blocks of time available are those for work or sleep. Do you want to sleep less or work less?

Look again at the subtitle of this book: "How to Achieve More by Working Less." You need to spend more time creating income-producing equity than you do now. You need to let your equity work for you, so you can have more time for other things. If you do it right, you can work less, sleep more, and still have time for a longer vacation, a relaxed meal, and time with your family.

MUST do to win.

1. Get a dream
2. Give your job a break and get off the Fast Track at work
3. Create a personal business
4. Create income-producing equity
5. Retire on Mentor Equity

You'll learn how to go through these steps as you progress through this book. It will be fun, and certainly more rewarding, than winning the lottery. In overcoming Time Poverty, you will grow personally. You will have choices. You can choose to spend your time doing anything you like.

If you do these things, you will live a different life than you do now. You will have time for the things that are most important. You will have a lifetime of income, without a lifetime of work.

When it comes time to retire, you will still have a fulfilling lifestyle. People will value your opinion and will want to be around you. You won't have to "give up" your life's work. You will still be involved, creative, energetic and excited about each and every day.

Best of all, you will be able to retire young. Or, you can keep your job and still have the time you need to enjoy yourself.

What Floats Your Boat?

My wife, Jeanne, and I have already done it. I have a job. I am a college professor, but each year we take long vacations. We have our own business and investment properties that produce even more income.

Our two daughters can attend any university they want. We have the money to help others and to make their lives better.

All this happened to us because we started playing a different game. And, all THAT started because I saw that boat on July 7, 1993. It woke me up and shook my world!

What will it be for you? It can be anything. Will you see a "boat" that rocks your world? Perhaps it will be this book. Perhaps it will be a friend who is a good example. Your "boat" might be a life-changing experience, or just a simple realization that you don't have what you want and you won't get it if you keep on doing what you're doing.

Folks, whatever it is, it will lead you to the same conclusion. The Work and Hope Game is mostly work—and very little hope! This book, and the system it describes, will replace that hope with help. I can help you get what you want, and you can help others.

Keep on reading, and let's play the right game!

Chapter 2

The Balance Game

I am definitely going to take a course in
time management—just as soon as I can
work it into my schedule.

— Louis E. Boone

A Typical Day

Let's look at a typical day for many middle-class people. The alarm goes off early. You and your spouse get out of bed. Neither of you got enough sleep last night. You spent many hours tossing and turning as thoughts of your busy day, your financial situation, the kids' school schedule, and other time-wrecking activities flooded your sleeping brain into semi-wakefulness.

You get the coffee on. (Imagine how tough your mornings would be without the stimulation of caffeine!) You get the kids out of bed and discover that little Joey needs a special binder for his school project.

All this initial hurry and worry leads to breakfast. Is it a relaxed family meal, a mellow beginning to another exciting day of family accomplishments? No. Breakfast in most households today is a hurried affair that, at best, resembles feeding time at the zoo. At worst, it's merely tossing a couple of dollars to each family member so they can slam down some greasy fast food before the day really starts.

Then everyone has jobs or school. The kids are out of the house, in someone else's care. Even the preschoolers are in day care. Both parents go to their jobs, where someone tells them how they will spend their time that day, just like every other work day.

Time Out – Whatever Happened to Recess?

My daughters attend a really fine public school. My kids' school always ranks among the top in the state. In fact, the school receives an "A+" rating each and every year.

But, they don't have recess!

Oh sure, my kids have PE (Physical Education), but that is a well-organized, step-by-step series of games and exercises. In fact, much of their time is spent sitting while the PE instructor reviews rules, techniques, etc!

When *I* was in grade school, we would gulp down our lunches and then have at least a half hour of recess. For my kids, lunch is different. They get about 25 minutes to eat, and then go right back to class to sit at a desk.

Whatever happened to recess? We traded it for efficiency. It seems like, today, we just can't stand to see people relaxing. Everything must be scheduled. It is no wonder that people are running out of time. They spend their entire childhoods learning how to meet a schedule.

Let's learn to play again. This advice goes for adults, too. Recreation helps build relationships, refreshes us and makes us happy. Try it!

At the end of another routine day, it is time to start the real merry-go-round of driving the kids to all the over-planned activities that substitute for play time and recreation. In today's society, we don't trust kids to come up with imaginative play time. We have to give them *structured* time—time that leads to more learning and developing so that they can get into the right school and get a good job and start this whole time-starved process with *their* families.

Does the day involve a nice, home-cooked dinner? Not likely! Recent studies show that almost 90% of meals are not prepared at home anymore. Can you imagine a time when your family could sit down to a home-cooked meal? Who would cook it? Who would be there to eat it? Who would have the time to clean up after it?

After dinner, or whatever substituted for it this day, it is time for homework and, of course, television. Yes, the ever-present, ever-running, television. After all, tonight is Tuesday, and on Tuesday, we all have to watch—well, there's going to be something on we can watch, right?

A few more struggles, a few more emergencies over special things the kids need for school tomorrow. Your report for work is due soon and your boss wants you to come in early. And you need to iron some clothes for the kids, do the wash, make lunches, and on and on it goes.

Finally, it is time for you to go to bed. But wait! There is a special guest on the late show! Oh well, you can always get some sleep this weekend.

Does all this sound familiar? It seems like almost everyone is experiencing Time Poverty. What happened? Didn't most of us grow up in a house that had more time? Didn't our parents make us home cooked meals? When we got sick at school, wasn't there someone home who could come and get us?

The truth is that most people *are* in time trouble. It isn't something we are just imagining. The average person barely has time to breathe, and it isn't getting any better. In fact, it looks like it will get even worse in the years to come.

The Myth of Balance

So where's the "balance" in this hectic schedule? Most people really don't know what they mean when they say "I want more balance in my life." They are so far removed from a balanced life that they have no concept of what they are wishing for.

Here is the first thing you need to know about balance: *It is a myth!* You can't balance your life at the level you are currently living!

You can't balance your life if you haven't got the means to balance it. You can't balance your family on one side of a seesaw if the weight of the debt that you have is on the other! By doing the things we often do—trading time for dollars and then using those dollars to buy stuff that has no future value—we are creating a monster that will never be balanced against our personal lives.

The only thing most people ever get into balance is their checkbook. Once a month they take their bank statements and see if they can figure out exactly what the heck happened! They look at the final balance and say, "Where did all the money go?"

But, at least you know what balance is! It is when one side of something is equal to the other. It is when you get out exactly what you put in.

How Do You Find Balance?

There are many articles in current magazines that talk about balance. They have titles like "Balancing Work and Family" or "Balancing Work and Relationships" or "Balancing Work and Leisure." In every case, WORK is on one side of the balance sheet. So, when most people today think about balancing their lives, they think about reducing the amount of work they do.

There is one big problem with this. If you reduce the work, you reduce the pay. If you reduce the pay, you reduce your choices. Soon, you have more time, but you are broke. So you have to work more to pay your bills, and soon you are out of balance again.

What's wrong with this thinking? We are thinking poor! We can't imagine how to increase our wealth by working less. We try to balance our lives by doing less work, making less money, and doing fewer things we enjoy. The problem is that *people try to balance their lives at the wrong level*, a LOWER lifestyle level. Instead they should balance their lives at a much HIGHER lifestyle level.

Balancing at a Higher Lifestyle Level

I am not surprised that people don't understand the concept of balancing their life at a higher lifestyle level. Almost every source of information is telling a different story. For example, do teachers show us how to have a fabulous lifestyle? No, they teach us how to "get the skills to work for a well established company." Do politicians lead us to have exciting and fulfilling lives? No, they ask us to vote for them because they will help create "good paying jobs." Do our friends encourage us to pursue our dreams? No, our friends are too busy trying to keep their own lives together than to give us the encouragement we need.

From the time we are born until the time we die, we are unintentionally taught to be poor—both financially poor and time poor. So, when I say "balance your life at a higher lifestyle level", many people have no idea what that means. We can't imagine how to live well. We can't imagine how to do anything else except what everyone else is doing.

I have friends who work hard at their jobs, with little time to spare. I really like these people. But it is hard to do things with them because they usually don't have time! But I also have friends that have lots of time and lots of money. These are the people I like to hang around with. I see myself in these people. I *think* the way they do.

The Message From the Media

The concept of *thinking* like time and money rich people is incredibly important. How do you see yourself? Are you an average person, who will live and die average? Or are you a wealthy person, who deserves to live well, with lots of time? Most people just don't think of themselves as anything but average.

Let me give you one example of why that happens. The media, especially television, reinforces all those stereotypes. They have shows *for* average people. But, they have shows *about* wealthy people. Did you ever notice that? All the advice shows and "special" news segments are supposed to be for the benefit of average people, and all the shows that feature great lifestyles are about the wealthy people.

A local television news station had a week-long series called "How to Live Cheaper." Who wants to live cheaper? I want to live BETTER! Anyway, one segment was "How to be Absolutely Stinking Cheap at a Restaurant." (Okay, it wasn't exactly called that, but it *was* about dining out at a lower cost.) Two pieces of advice really made me crazy. The first was, "Eat a lot of bread at the table so you won't order as much food." The other bit of advice was, "Go to a really nice restaurant for a romantic lunch rather than a romantic dinner, because it costs less."

I don't know about you, but I don't go to a really nice restaurant for the bread. I go for the food! I go for the atmosphere! I go with my wife for the candlelit tables! If you are so cheap that you take your sweetheart to lunch in the middle of the afternoon because you don't want to spend the money for dinner in the evening, then she or he should leave you for someone with money!

The point is this—you shouldn't balance your life by cutting back. You should balance it by moving forward. Forget what everyone is telling you. Don't balance at a low lifestyle level, balance at a high lifestyle level by working less and making more!

So, what about the programs that show the wealthy? How about *Lifestyles of the Rich and Famous*? Check out *Great Vacation Homes*. What about those travel shows to far away exotic islands? Those shows are all *about* wealthy people, aren't they? Did any of those people become wealthy by eating rolls before dinner?

You can try balancing your life by cutting back on work, or expenditures. But, what kind of life will you have? What kind of lessons will you pass on to your children?

Why not become one of the wealthy? Why not choose a path that increases your income *and* your time, so you can achieve balance at a higher lifestyle level?

Five years from now, which television show will you be featured on? Will it be *A Cheap Miser Who Eats Dinner at Lunch*, or *Lifestyles of Time-Rich People*?

Get Out of Balance First

I hate to tell you this, but you may have to get even MORE out of balance in order to make some changes. You may have to work even harder—at least for a while—in order to straighten out that see-saw at a level that gives you a more balanced lifestyle.

There is an old saying, "If you want to make an omelet, you have to break some eggs." I like to think of it a little differently. "If you want to make an omelet, you have to get a little scrambled!"

My friends John and Julie are great examples of people who got a little "scrambled" in order to make a fantastic lifestyle. John was a home builder and Julie was a teacher when they decided they just weren't getting the things they wanted. Sure, they had some money, a nice home and lots of friends. But they couldn't really enjoy it because they were so busy with work and other obligations.

John and Julie made a decision that would have scared most couples to death. Actually, as Julie tells it, "It frightened me so much I couldn't even let myself think about it at first. I just went through the motions."

What did they do? They partnered with some friends to create a personal business that distributed products directly to consumers. Then, they took the proceeds from that business to create investments that *paid them more money*. Was it crazy for a while? "Yes," says John. "But, we realized that we had to go OUT OF BALANCE if we were going to have what we wanted."

John and Julie are now in their mid-40's. They spend lots of time with their children, taking family vacations at their resort home. Julie left teaching shortly after they started their personal business, and John left his company a few years later. Today, they have cut way back on their work in their personal business, and they plan to retire fully in another three years. What will they do after retirement? They will visit their investment properties, speak to groups of entrepreneurs, move full-time to their vacation home and spend time with their family.

How long were John and Julie out of balance? As John recalls, "It was hard work when we started the distribution network, but it was very rewarding. After five years of really going crazy, we had it all—time, money and the friends to spend a lifestyle with."

Sound good? Go get scrambled and create your own omelet.

How Will You Play the Balance Game?

So, how will you play the game? Will you try to balance everything at the present level by cutting back on work, income, choices and lifestyle? Or, will you break out of the rut you have been in and have a wealthy, happy, stress-free life with lots of time to do the things you want most? Is this the day you make that decision?

The outcomes of your balance game will depend a lot on who you play the game with. If you want to become an outstanding golfer, playing on championship courses throughout the world, do you look for a partner who tours only on miniature golf courses? Or do you play with someone who aspires to the same level you do?

Folks, play the balance game with people who are balanced at a level you would like to attain! Stop thinking about cutting back, and start thinking about LIVING! You need both time and money. If your current game style isn't producing that for you, you need to make a change—now.

Chapter 3

Bottlenecks: The Sports and Corporate Games

Two men were watching the Tour de France, a grueling, three-week bicycle race. The riders must race their bikes up steep mountains, around curves and over many miles of country roads and city streets. The race covers more than 2,100 miles!

The first man said, "I don't understand why these guys would go through this terrible ordeal."

"Well," said the second man. "The winner gets a lot of money and is a celebrity. He lives a fabulous lifestyle."

"Oh, I understand why the winner would do it," said the first man. "I just don't understand why all those other guys would go through with it!"

I feel the same way. I can understand why the winners go through all the pain and suffering. They get wealth, fame and fortune. But why would all those other people go through the pain? They will never get the rewards that are equal to their efforts!

The Sports Game and the "Bottleneck"

Unlike the majority of the bike riders in the Tour de France, many top athletes make fabulous amounts of money for playing their sport. They also make thousands more through lucrative endorsements. But for every top sports professional, there are thousands of players who will never make a dime from the sport. Just like our bike riders, they will never get the rewards that are equal to the effort.

Yet, in every playground, on every court and at every golf club, you will find countless numbers of young people who dream of playing sports professionally.

Of course, very few of these young people will play professional sports. Some just don't have the talent or physical attributes to make the grade. And, even if they have the physical gifts, a professional career requires athletes to SACRIFICE countless hours and days, even years of their lives. Did Tiger Woods become one of the world's best, and richest, golfers by simply buying a nice set of clubs? No, he sacrificed!

To get a good idea of the odds against a young man or woman becoming a top athlete, imagine a large glass bottle, wide at the bottom, with a long, thin neck. There are thousands of athletes in the bottle, but only a few will "pop" out the top as superstars.

And here is the problem. Many of the rest of those athletes who were almost as good also spent their lives trying to make it. They too gave up months and years in an effort to "strike it rich" through sports.

In the end, what did they have to show for it? Not much. Maybe they made some money. Maybe all they ever got were some trophies or awards. If they were staking it all on a sports career and they didn't make it, they had very little indeed.

So What Do We Tell Young People?

As parents, teachers and counselors, we often say, "Don't put all your efforts into a professional sports career. The chances are you will never attain it. Instead, have fun playing sports and get a good education. That way, you will always be able to get a good job."

But we are wrong!

We aren't wrong that it is unlikely they will have a career in professional sports. We aren't wrong when we tell them to have fun with sports. And, we certainly aren't wrong when we tell them that only a very few people will ever become superstars.

But, we *are* wrong when we tell them to get a good education so they can get a job!

From One Game to Another

Why are we wrong when we tell people that a job is the key to success? Because the chances of becoming a *top player* in the corporate world are just as slim as becoming a top professional athlete! And, unlike athletic superstars, corporate superstars don't get to retire at thirty-five. Corporate superstars have to work until they are too old to work anymore.

We are giving our young people the wrong advice. We are telling them to give up one futile game and to substitute another futile game. It is shocking!

I talked about sports as being a bottle, with a bottleneck at the top. Only a few people "pop" out of the top of the bottle as superstars. The same analogy applies to the Corporate Game.

Millions of people work unbelievably hard, trying to move up the corporate ladder. Only a tiny number of those hard-working people will ever "pop" out of the neck of that bottle. Many of the others will work almost as hard, will give up their family lives, will pin their hopes on a top salary and stock options, and will trade all their time in search of that elusive "superstar" spot in the corporate world—the CEO.

In the corporate world, the struggle goes on for 40 or 50 years. By the time you give it up, you are old! And you have spent your life trading away your time.

When someone fails at the Sports Game, he or she is still young. Imagine, for example, a 12-year-old who discovers the game of baseball. He joins a Little League team and becomes one of the stars. He plays all through high school, and even wins a scholarship to college. He is later drafted by a professional team.

Our young man spends three years in the minor leagues, playing in small ball parks for a small salary. He works hard, hoping to be called up to the major leagues. One day, he gets his chance.

In the majors, however, the game is completely different. Our player gives it everything he has, but he never really makes it big. Although he is one of the hardest workers his coaches have ever seen, they have to let him go.

Our boy is cut from the team and his career is over. He is twenty-six. What can he do now?

Well, he can do almost anything! He is only twenty-six. He had a fantastic experience! He has learned a great deal about life already. Now he can take that experience and use it to produce a wealthy lifestyle. He has the whole world ahead of him.

The Corporate Game

What about his friends who didn't play professional sports? They played the Corporate Game. After college, they entered the workforce, where they started to learn the rules of a different game. They begin to see that the competition gets a lot stiffer as they climb the corporate ladder.

These young people soon learn something else about the Corporate Game—it's not as much fun as the Sports Game. Most professional athletes love the game they are playing. They wish they could go on playing it for the rest of their lives. Yes, it is a lot of hard work, but they are doing what they love to do.

How many players in the Corporate Game can say that? How many players say, "I wish this would go on forever!"?

Time Poverty and the Corporate Game

By now, you may be saying to yourself, "Wow, I never thought about the Corporate Game like that, but what does it have to do with getting more time in my life?"

It has everything to do with it. If you spend your time doing the wrong things—depending on the Corporate Game to give you a lifestyle—you are spending a lifetime giving away your time. And along the way, you are being sent some clear messages. Here are a few.

Message 1—Spend money

I am always reminded of one of my students from the University of Nevada, Las Vegas (UNLV). Joel was a bright guy who got a great job upon graduation. He was hired as a consultant by a national company.

The day after Joel's graduation, my wife and I went to an electronics store to buy something. There was Joel, buying the BIGGEST stereo system I had ever seen.

Was he paying cash for it? Of course not. He was buying it on credit. However, he was going from making almost no money as a student, to making a nice salary as a consultant-trainee. He was going to spend that money as soon as he could. After all, he had put off buying things for four years!

Message 2—Work hard to get a promotion

Soon, you learn a second lesson. Work harder than other people and you will get a promotion. With a promotion comes a raise. With a raise you can buy more stuff!

Of course, you buy those things on credit. But you pay for that credit by working more hours.

You are playing the Corporate Game. The problem is that you are trading more and more time for those dollars. You are losing time, not gaining wealth.

Message 3—Get on the Fast Track

In order to play the Corporate Game to its maximum, you get on the Fast Track. What is the Fast Track? It is the road to getting noticed and getting promoted. It is the road to more raises. It is the road to corporate commitment. It is the road to the top of the bottle, right to the bottleneck itself!

To be on the Fast Track, you need to be noticed. How? By

Time Out – The Boss's Mood?

I couldn't believe it. CNN, the most respected worldwide source for news, was telling people how to get a raise at their jobs. This story demonstrated just how far we have gone to sell our time to our bosses.

A consultant advised, "Make sure your boss is in a good mood when you ask for a raise. If you see that he or she is not happy, wait for another day to ask."

I was stunned! Imagine how terrible life is when you have to assess you boss's mood before asking for fair compensation!

Folks, if this is your situation, change it! Don't stake your financial future on the whim or personality of another person. You are better than that!

Follow the steps in this book and you will not have to worry about what mood your boss is in. Get off the Fast Track at work and get on the Leverage Track in a personal business.

Don't quit your job—just quit waiting for someone else to set you free.

doing more work than anyone else. You're the first one there in the morning and the last one to leave. You take work home and do it there. You give up weekends.

You are spending so much time trying to create a lifestyle that you have no life! And there is no end in sight. There is always some reason to spend more time working. It might be for the next promotion or raise. It might be to have that extra trip to Disney World. It might be for a new home. It might be for a very good reason.

It doesn't matter if the reason is good. The point is there is always a reason. There is always some reason to work harder, to spend more time.

Why is there no end in sight? Because, all along the way, raises are spent on *things*—a bigger home, or another car—on credit! Mortgages and loans trap you into this cycle. You can't stop!

And just like the Sports Game, it is very unlikely that you will emerge from the neck of the bottle. Most players in the Corporate Game—in fact, the vast majority—will never get out of the bottle. Oh, they will get ahead to some degree. But, they will spend a lifetime of extremely hard work. They will give up so much of their time. They will let another person dictate their schedule. They will trade so much for the dream of having more—only to find that they can't have more by doing what they have been doing.

Message 4—Wait until you retire to enjoy life

Even if you're not on the Fast Track, your schedule is still dictated by your job. But you are looking forward to retiring after a long lifetime of work. You are planning on the days when you will have all the time *and* money you need to do all the things you have wanted to do all these years.

But it doesn't work that way. There is no rainbow at the end of the Corporate Game for most people. Studies show that the average person working today will retire at less than $20,000 in annual income. Most people who retire today will live on Social Security. Why? Because they spent all their money on stuff—good or bad—that did not produce an income for them. Sure, they have a nice house that is worth some money. But, the vast majority of people in the workforce today have re-financed their homes to pay off credit card debts, or school loans, or cars, or something. Then, they got into more debt.

So when they retire, they don't have the money to do the things they wanted to do. They lose their primary source of income, but not their debts!

And when they retire, many people have a sense of loss because they spent a lifetime in the Corporate Game, and don't have much of a life outside of work. Many people are so wrapped in the status of their careers that they really do not have another identity.

But I Own a Small Business!

If you are self-employed, you may not be any better off than someone who plays the Corporate Game. A recent survey by the magazine *Fortune Small Business* found that the average small business is open 11 hours per day, six days per week. Small business owners and the self-employed are still trading time for dollars. If they stop working, the business stops, the money stops and the creditors start calling.

Many small business people simply "buy" their jobs. They say, "I work for myself. There is no boss telling me what to do." But, just like the employees at a larger company, the self-employed cannot simply take off whenever they feel like it. They need the money that they get by being available for their customers. They trade one boss for a whole lot of bosses!

What Can I Do About All This?

The first step is to realize that you can't win a lifestyle by playing the Corporate Game. You can make money. You can even make a LOT of money. But you will never have the time to really enjoy it.

Don't get me wrong. I'm not telling you to quit your job in order to gain time. In fact, in the next chapter, you'll see there is a lot to be gained by having a job you really like. Just don't fool yourself into thinking it will give you a great lifestyle. Working in the Corporate Game *can* give you security, friendships and a great place to learn about business. You are going to need all those things as you build a Time-Rich life.

In the coming chapters, you are going to learn how to build equity that produces an incredible income OUTSIDE your job. You will learn how to gain time and wealth by playing a different game—a game that anyone can win.

Chapter 4

Winning the Work Game

No man goes before his time—unless the boss leaves early.

— Groucho Marx

Kenny Rogers, the famous Country & Western singer and businessman, received some interesting advice from his mother.

She said, "If you do something you love, you will never work a day in your life."

It is easy to see what she meant. People who love their jobs don't consider them work! If you have a passion for your job, if it is really interesting and challenging, if you get a real sense of accomplishment when you complete a task, then it really doesn't seem like you are working.

Finding a job that you love is essential in overcoming Time Poverty. Yet, not many people really love their work. They look at their work as just some way to get what they want. That wouldn't be so bad if you really *could* get what you want from a job.

What Do You Want From Work?

If you have a fundamental knowledge of what motivates people to work, then the task of understanding what people want from their work becomes simpler. People operate in some fairly predictable ways. Almost everyone is on a *journey* that leads them in a search for basic necessities first, then for more spiritual achievements later.

Think of the difference between a child and a teenager. The child is happy with uncomplicated things. Give a child a balloon, or a new toy, and he or she is happy. But a teenager is on the search for new experiences, more complicated fulfillments.

Now, imagine an adult who is looking for fulfillment. An adult isn't happy with the things that satisfy a teenager! A teenager may find his or her complete identity in a nice car. An adult wants the nice car, of course, but he or she also want a nice home, a job with status, and so forth. A teenager may take a really terrible job for the sole purpose of buying a car. An adult views the job differently. They see it as their career.

What does all this mean? It means that people move from one stage to another throughout their lives. The things we look for from work develop and change as we grow. While we first take a job just to make ends meet, we soon want other things, more sophisticated things. And the more we have, the more we want.

Maslow's Hierarchy of Needs

This process of development, of moving from simple needs to more complicated needs, was observed by a man named Abraham Maslow. Anyone who has ever taken a course in human motivation has heard of Maslow. He stated that people spend their entire lives trying to satisfy a changing and growing series of needs.

Maslow described how people operate in what is commonly called a hierarchy. In other words, they start out wanting fundamental or basic things: air, water, food, clothing and shelter. After going through this first stage, they move on.

The second stage involves creating security and safety. Once those needs are met, people enter the third stage, where they look for a sense of belonging. They look for people like themselves. (What is the problem with finding people just like you? Well, if you surround yourself with people just like you, and those people are not successful, you will all stay at the same level for the rest of your life!)

The fourth stage is the ego stage. Here, men and women do things, buy things and try things that make them feel important.

Finally, a few people reach the stage of self-actualization. One author described self-actualization in terms of the United States' Army's slogan, "Be all you can be." A self-actualized person is one who is looking for fulfillment. They have gone through the processes of making a living. Now, they can make a life.

Your Job and Your Career

While many people search for fulfillment from their jobs, most are not that happy with their work. They are not achieving a sense of self-actualization from what they do. And they do what they do *for 49 hours per week* on average! They do what they do, day in and day out, for forty to fifty years! And they can't wait until retirement so they can STOP.

Maybe *your* job isn't so bad. Maybe you *love* what you do and would do it for free if they stopped paying you. Maybe you would not trade one day on your job for all the money and time in the world. If you are one of those people—GREAT! But if you are like most people, you spend much of your time at a job that is, at best, somewhat satisfying, and at worst, a real pain in the neck!

For an interesting experiment in human behavior, try going to lunch at a place frequented by business people. Sit somewhere where you can hear the conversations at nearby tables.

What will you hear? People will be complaining about their bosses, or co-workers, or some other problem at work. People are passionate about their jobs, but, for the most part, they see themselves as under-appreciated, surrounded by co-workers and systems that are specifically designed to make their life harder!

You hardly ever hear about the great sense of fulfillment someone is getting, or the terrific rewards that are pouring in from their job.

Do Something You Love Instead

Suppose you work for the post office, but you do carpentry projects in your basement for fun. If you are not all that crazy about your job at the post office, why shouldn't you quit and become a carpenter full time?

Suppose you really like golf. Why don't you leave your job as a pharmaceutical salesman and sell golf clubs for a living? Wouldn't you love to take clients to the golf course, fit them for custom clubs and then play a round or two with them?

Time Out – I Want to Be a Firefighter

Kids know a great job when they see it. In their minds, a great job has action, excitement, great uniforms, and the chance to work with really cool equipment. You know the kind of equipment I mean—the stuff that looks like big toys.

What do kids want to be when they grow up? Firefighters, police, crane operators, pilots, dancers, singers, and so forth.

Each year, my wife and I go to my daughter's school to give a talk on "Career Day." We get a lot of great questions from the kids. And we always ask them, "What would you like to be?" In five years, after talking with hundreds of kids, not one of them ever said, "I want to be a clerk in a large municipal office." No one has ever expressed their desire to be an economist, a tax consultant, or an insurance salesman.

I am not saying anything bad about these jobs. What I am saying is that most of us take jobs for the money and not because we love them. A lot of work that people do is boring, yet they keep doing it because they don't know what else to do.

After reading this book, you will have a choice. Do you want to spend the rest of your life doing something that you don't really enjoy just to get some money? Do you really want to give up almost one third of your total time for a job?

Overcoming Time Poverty is a process, not a job. So, do the things necessary to achieve your dreams. Get a dream, do a job you like, have a business of your own, and invest the profits into equity-building assets.

And the next time you hear the fire alarm go off, put your boots on and slide down the pole!

Some people actually do this, and I am not opposed to it. Certainly, from a Time Poverty viewpoint, a radical change like this can solve a lot of problems for you. You wouldn't feel so much pressure on your time if you were going off to do something you really liked.

But the reality is that most people don't have something they really like to do that much. Sometimes doing something you really like is not that much fun if you *have* to do it. I *love* fishing, but it wouldn't be as much fun if I had to get up every day, go out to the boat, and start catching and cleaning fish to support my family.

Most people would find it really hard to say they love their jobs.

They may like their jobs. It might even be a lot of fun at times. *But most people are looking for something from their jobs that a job just isn't designed to give them.* Now, if you can stop asking more of your job than it is meant to give, you will find that you can enjoy your work more. You will find that your job is just a small part of your journey for wealth and time.

So, here we are, right back where we started—trying to find something you love doing. The trick is not to look at yourself as your job or your career. Look at yourself as someone who has a high purpose in life. Look at yourself—and just as importantly— look at others as people who are on the road to time and wealth freedom.

Give Everyone a Break

Time Out – Become the "B" Employee

The *Harvard Business Review* has run some great articles describing the benefits of being a "B" employee. But who are these "B" employees? They are the "worker bees" who like their jobs and like the company they work for. "B" employees are not looking for a promotion. They don't want to work extra hours. They value non-work time and realize they would have to give up too much to move up in the company.

"A" employees are different. They stand out and are the stars. Their ambition is to move up, level by level, until they are running the show. "A" employees may not like their jobs as much, because they are using those jobs only as stepping stones.

Harvard Business Review pointed out the benefits of being a "B" employee to both the worker and the company. "B" employees have lower stress and are more content. Surprisingly, when companies need to lay people off, the "A" employees are more likely to go. It turns out that most companies depend on "B" employees to keep everything running.

You will read this lesson again and again in this book: do a great job, but get off the Fast Track. Make a living from your work-time, but make a life from your non-work time!

You have been asking your boss for too much. You want him or her to understand you and your special needs, but your boss doesn't have time for that. There is a business to run.

So take the pressure off your boss. Do a great job, but just do *your* job. It is not your boss's responsibility to get your whole life in order. You will take care of your life. YOU are the only one responsible for it.

Give your boss a break. Relax, and you will find a whole new attitude at work—yours and the boss'!

If you're a boss, give your employees a break. Most managers are going to have a hard time with this idea. They are going to think, "I don't want my people thinking about anything else but their jobs. I want them to be here for as long as it takes to get the job done. I want them to listen to me and do what I say."

But in the very near future, I believe that many managers will begin to see the value of an employee who doesn't *need* the job. They will see the benefit of having employees whose jobs fill *part* of their financial and self-worth needs.

Think about it. Who would make a better employee—someone who is having a bad day but comes to work anyway so they can get paid, or someone who is living a great life and who loves his or her work?

Bosses, give your people a break! Don't expect them to find fulfillment on the job. They need to find fulfillment in life, and the job can be a great part of that process.

Give Your Job a Break

How does this relate to Time Poverty? Put your job back into perspective. Give it a break. Fit your job into your life—not your life into your job.

Think of Maslow. Use your job to satisfy your basic needs, but don't look there for self-actualization. Your job simply isn't going to give you that level of rewards. Cover the basics at work, but use your free time to find true fulfillment.

Most importantly, get off the Fast Track at work. It is only a Fast Track to increased stress and Time Poverty. Don't look for promotions, more responsibility, and overtime. Look for a position you like and one that you can handle. Then, start looking for fulfillment *outside* work.

This change will make a huge difference in your time, because it will make a huge difference in your income, your attitude, and your relationships.

Time and the Fast Track—My Experience

Let me tell you about my personal experience with the Fast Track. As you know, I am a college professor. Now, there is a rumor that professors don't make much money, but it doesn't have to be true. I have created a lifestyle that gives me both time *and* money. And, I did it by following my own advice. I have a primary source of income—the university where I teach—and personal businesses that produce the REAL money. Of course, it didn't happen overnight! But, my lifestyle is great. There is plenty of time and money.

My exit from the Fast Track started years ago when I decided to get out of the corporate world and go back to school for my Ph.D. There is no question. I was on the Fast Track early on. I owned and operated a hotel at the age of 19, and a restaurant at 20. Later, I became a Food & Beverage Director at a ski resort in Lake Tahoe.

I was putting in many hours on the job. That was okay when I was younger and just learning the business world. But, as I got a little more experience, I could see that the job market was just not going to give me the time I wanted. That is when I went back to school.

But even at a university there is a Fast Track. You see, the only way that most college professors can make more money is to stop teaching and become an administrator. The real money is at the level of a Dean, Vice-President or President. So, many professors leave the relatively stress free life of a professor, where they have classes two days per week, to work five or six days per week as an administrator.

That life was not for me! I didn't want to work for someone else any more hours than I had to. Long ago, I decided to remain a professor, even though I was approached several times to apply for a Dean's job. I took myself off the Fast Track at work. I wasn't willing to give up the free time that comes with being a professor. And I didn't want to look to the University to find true fulfillment.

How Anyone Can Play the Work Game

It is easy to play the work game, if you take it easy at work! Don't look for *all* of your personal fulfillment at work. It won't be there. And, if it is, you are missing a whole lot of life.

Play the work game to get the basics. You will be happier, believe me. You don't need a job to get the really good things in life. In fact, your job will NEVER give you the really good things.

The problem is, we spend so much time at work that we think it HAS to be the most important tool for personal satisfaction. For example, in his new book, Jack Welch, the retired CEO of General Electric, talks about how great it was to go to work *each Saturday*. And, he talked about how he expected each of his managers to be there too!

Donald Trump is also very fulfilled at work. Why not? He owns the company and is very wealthy. But, how excited are the people who work for him? Do they all share in his deep sense of accomplishment?

Folks, get a job you like and do it well. But, build your sense of worth outside the job. Gain time freedom by shedding your dependence on someone else. Play the game to win at life, not win at work.

Chapter 5

The Retirement Game

Time is a great healer, but a poor beautician.

— Lucille S. Harper

The major reason people are Time-Poor is simple. They work too much. They are willing to spend so much time at work because they believe that one day, they can retire and have all the time they want. But why wait? You don't have to be old to retire. You just need a new plan.

The Trouble with Traditional Retirement

Here it is. The time of your life. You have been planning on this time for the last twenty years. You and your spouse will finally get to do all the things you couldn't do while you were working. There will be no boss to tell you what to do. You are the master of your own time. Finally!

But there are three main problems with traditional retirement. First, most people retire in their 60's or later. Wouldn't they have enjoyed more time when they were younger? Second, it is something completely new to them. They have to learn what to do with their days now that they are not working. Third, their income has stopped! Now they have time, but are busy protecting their assets. They are on the dreaded "fixed income."

Let's talk about these three problems:

If You Wait Until Your Sixties, Life Passes You By

Tom and Mary Wilton live in Tampa, Florida. Tom is the regional manager for an automobile parts company. He has worked very hard, moving up the corporate ladder and moving locations four times. Tom is now 63 and is seriously thinking about retirement. However, he has one son still in school and he has a lot of debt. He plans to work for "a few more years."

Mary would also like to retire. She is two years younger than Tom and has worked most of her life. She took a few years off when her three boys were very young, but the Wiltons needed money for the kids' education, so she went back to work.

Both Tom and Mary view retirement as a time when they can stop doing all the things they no longer want to do—mainly go to work. They have each worked for over 40 years. During that time, they missed school plays, vacations, and dinners with each other.

How does Tom view retirement? Well, here are his words:

"I am going to shoot my alarm clock and give away all my ties. I am going to get my golf clubs out and play, play, play!"

Mary adds, "I am going to do all the things I haven't had time to do. I also want to take some trips with Tom. We haven't had a decent vacation in years. I think we might go on a cruise."

Does that sound familiar? It should. Tom and Mary are typical. They look at retirement as a time to stop doing what they were doing. In the next twenty years, they're going to try to make up for all the things they didn't have time for in the last forty.

When the Job Stops, There Goes Your Identity

My father called me today while I was writing. He asked how the book was coming along.

"I am doing a chapter on retirement," I said. "Do you have any thoughts?"

"Yeah," he said. "I just got back from the barber shop and met George Dimoto there. You remember him, don't you?"

I knew George. He was a great guy. He had a great job. He had socked away a fair amount of money during his work career. He had a lot of friends and played a great game of golf.

"George said he was playing golf four to five times a week

since he retired two months ago. He is really worried. This is August. He is worried about what he is going to do to fill his days when it gets cold and his golf course closes!"

So, there was George, a victim of retirement's "before and after" syndrome. Before retirement, George was very busy with his job, with meetings, and so forth. He had respect, status and money. Now, he is just another retired guy, playing golf.

That's the trouble with traditional retirement. One day you are a big shot whose opinion really matters, the next day you are out of the loop—just some guy who plays a lot of golf and gets senior citizen discounts.

The Dreaded "Fixed" Income

How many times have you seen people on television complaining about the cost of prescription drugs? They say, "When medication prices go up, it is very hard for people on fixed incomes," or "I am on a fixed income so I have to watch what I spend."

What is a fixed income? It is an income that never goes up. If you are getting the same amount every month—from a pension or from Social Security—the amount is fixed. In other words, no matter what you do, you can never make more money.

Retired people on a fixed income spend a lot of their time trying to protect the money and equity they have. They go to sales, look all over the place for early-bird specials and cut back on all the things they wanted to do.

They have gone from a situation where they had money, but no time, to a situation where they have plenty of time, but limited money. And, it took them forty years of hard work to get there!

So What's the Alternative?

When you learn to "play the game" the right way, you learn to create a lifestyle that starts early and lasts a lifetime! Imagine this—you have a job that you really enjoy, and you build a thriving personal business on the side. Over time, you invest the profits of your business back into the business and into equity-producing investments such as real estate. Eventually, your assets and personal business produce enough income for you to leave your job.

Time Out – Forced Retirement

In recent years, thousands of Americans have lost their jobs due to outsourcing: the process of using foreign nationals on foreign soil to do jobs such as customer service. According to the AARP, over 540,000 American jobs went overseas in 2004.

Many blue-collar jobs have been sent overseas. An article in AARP Magazine describes the near-empty parking lot of a Johnson and Johnson plant in North Brunswick, New Jersey when hundreds of its high-paying jobs were moved to Brazil.

The article quotes a former employee with more than 30 years with the company: "It's devastating. Most of us won't find jobs making the money we make now."

And the chances of an older worker finding a new job are slim to begin with. When a 30-year veteran goes on a job hunt, he is very unlikely to find a company that will hire him at the same rate, with the same seniority and benefits. Companies today are looking for younger workers, who are more energetic and more likely to put in the time the company wants.

Let's learn a lesson from this man. If he had spent the past 30 years building a personal business to make additional money, and invested that money in assets that built equity, he would probably have an entirely different attitude.

As the saying goes, "Dig the well before you need the water!"

Now, you are retired! *But, you are younger than most retirees.* How young? It depends on how old you are when you learn to play the right game and how much effort you put into it. When you do retire from your job, you are still building your personal business. You are still buying assets. You are still creating wealth.

However, you can golf, fish or travel whenever you want. You can always put your business on hold for a little while, because you have sought out and trained other people who are also playing the right game.

Instead of retiring and sitting around with other retired people, you are still involved with younger, working people. They look to you for your advice, expertise, and friendship. You teach your children how to play the game, and they have time to spend time with you.

Your wealth continues to grow, you grow personally and your

relationships strengthen. You have won the game.

When Do I Get To Retire?

My wife and I were first exposed to Time-Rich people at a business meeting in 1991. They shared their stories and talked about business opportunities. It seemed like hard work.

However, there is a big difference between working hard for yourself and working hard for someone else.

What Jeanne and I have learned is that most people retire because they want to stop doing the things they don't want to do. We are on a different track. We are not on the Fast Track in the Corporate Game. We, like many people we know and admire, are playing a totally different game.

Jeanne and I don't intend to retire in the traditional sense. Like the people we most admire, we plan to continue doing exactly what we are doing now—owning a personal business, helping other people learn how to build wealth,

Time Out – Living for the Weekends

Juan and Carolina enjoy their lives—two days per week. Both are highly educated professionals. Carolina is a nurse administrator for a research clinic. Juan works for the government. They put in long hours and take home work at night.

"We live for the weekends," says Carolina. "Those are *our* days. We give all the other time for work."

This couple has two problems, and they know it.

First, as Juan puts it, "When the weekend finally arrives, we are so busy that we don't have time to relax and enjoy it. We have to do all the things that we didn't have time to do during the week. We are always running to the store, doing errands, and taking care of chores around the house."

Even worse, the second problem has this couple extremely concerned. "The really scary part," says Juan "is that we will probably be doing this for the rest of our lives! I don't see an end in sight."

He is right. Unless they make some major changes, they will never get out of this race. They will spend their time working and waiting— waiting for retirement when they can stop working. But this couple has nothing to look forward to except living on Social Security and a small pension. It is time for a change!

continuing to build equity, and doing all the things we want to do right now—not waiting until another man tells me it is time to do them.

Jeanne and I have time—right now. We are Time-Rich, not Time-Poor—and so are the people we admire.

We have friends and family to spend our time with, and they are fabulous people. They are on the journey with us.

Retirement? Keep the gold watch. I am having too much fun!

Chapter 6

The Leverage Game— The Right Game

They say that time changes things, but you actually have to change them yourself.

— Andy Warhol

By now, I think you'll agree that most people are playing the wrong game. They're trying to balance their lives at the wrong lifestyle level. They warn their children about the dangers of the Sports Game, but cheer them on when they enter the Corporate Game. They spend a lifetime at work, looking for rewards that aren't there. And they discover that retirement is mostly a game of hanging out and hanging on.

Is there any good news?

Yes! There is some very good news. In fact, there is *great* news.

You can still be a winner, still be a superstar. You can have it all—wealth, time, meaningful work, as well as a lot of fun. It is time to play the right game—the Leverage Game.

In the Leverage Game, you can expect:

- to have a primary source of income from a job or profession that you like doing
- to create powerful, VALUABLE time
- to develop a business of your own
- to have the money and time to enjoy your life
- to develop strong relationships with family and friends
- to work with others to create wealth
- to become a master gamer who teaches others to succeed

- to enjoy a balanced, meaningful life
- to continue creating wealth, even after you retire
- to live a life that God intended for you

The Plan

Here is what your life should look like. Here is a "superstar" in the Leverage Game:

You have a job you really like. It provides a base income, with some security. You have a good health plan, or at least you are able to afford health insurance. You work with good people and you do something worthwhile.

You are definitely not on the Fast Track. Why? Because you know that there is no way to win by following the Fast Track. You are the very best at your job that you can be. You are not looking for advancement past a certain point, but you do a great job anyway, because you never want to endanger your primary source of income. You are confident in that knowledge, and that allows you to relax and to enjoy your job.

You create great dreams that raise the excitement in your life. Your dreams are powerful motivators. They drive you to make some extraordinary changes in your life. But, you know that your job will never help you achieve your dreams. Your dream is to have money and the time to spend it. Your dream is to be a master life-gamer who has time for family and friends, as well as time for your dreams.

You learn how to increase the value of your time by creating a self-owned business that delivers equity and continuing income. You take the lessons you learn from the Corporate Game and apply them to this business. Then, you take the lessons you learn from your own business and apply them to the Corporate Game.

As you build your own business, you enjoy extraordinary changes in your life. Your business builds and your income grows. You reinvest the profits in equity and income-producing assets.

Your assets are now producing as much wealth as your job. Your primary source of income still sustains your basic lifestyle, but your personal business is fulfilling two purposes—additional income and also ego fulfillment. You don't miss the Fast Track at work, because you are getting all the benefits of the Fast Track—and more!

You retire from your primary source of income—at the age *you* choose. Your income is still increasing. And, because you have reinvested in assets, you are not trading time for dollars. You have highly valuable time to spare!

Instead of trying to fill your retirement time with new hobbies, or taking on a low paying job just to make ends

Time Out – The Second Economy

Years ago, I saw a cartoon in a magazine that makes a great point. Two men in long white robes with halos over their heads were standing on a cloud. They were watching another man, similarly attired, driving a white convertible with piles of money in the back seat. One of the first men says to the other, "I just believed it when they said you can't take it with you!"

Folks, it is the same with having lots of time and money here. You have been *told* one thing. You make your money by trading your time for it. But the reality is there are *lots* of other ways to make money without giving up time. I call this the Second Economy. If you believe it when they tell you there is only one way to do things, you will be stuck in the First Economy, and you will miss many great opportunities.

In the Second Economy, you want to *add value*, and then keep a piece of that value. Learn to add speed or convenience, re-package information, unleash the power of hidden resources, and take advantage of new technology.

Look around. Products, services, information and *money* are flying by! Just learn to reach out and touch them. Don't reinvent the wheel; just learn to grease it a little!

Best of all, you can usually do this on your own time. Keep your job in the First Economy, but get your hand into the Second Economy. Learn to add value, and you will leverage your time and wealth.

meet, you are growing. Your income continues to grow. But, more importantly, you are growing personally and spiritually. You are teaching others to do what you did. Your life is full. You have the time to do what you want, the money to do what you want, and you are DOING what you want.

There is one big difference, however. "What you want" has changed. Instead of looking forward to retirement so that you can stop doing what you didn't want to do, you are looking forward to retirement because it is exciting, fulfilling and rewarding.

Why Teamwork Doesn't Work—Usually

Are you on a team at work? Does your boss always talk about teamwork? Did you ever wonder why teams don't work in traditional businesses?

Teamwork doesn't work because everyone is competing for a limited amount of positions and rewards. Stephen Covey, in his fantastic book *The Seven Habits of Highly Effective People*, said that there are two kinds of people in the world—those with a theory of scarcity and those with a theory of abundance. Scarcity folks are players in the Corporate Game. They assume that there is only so much to go around. They compete against other people—even people on their own teams. Why? Because they want more, and the only way to get more is to get it from someone else.

Abundance thinkers are different. They know that if there isn't enough of something right now, the best way to get more is to make more of it! Abundance thinkers aren't competing against others. They compete against themselves. They want to create more so that everyone can have more.

In the Leverage Game, you can work on a team where *everyone* gets what they want. You can work with other people to help them get what they want and still have plenty for you! In fact, in the Leverage Game, if you run out of something, you work together to make more.

What is the Leverage Game?

In the Corporate Game, players are limited to the results of their individual efforts. The Corporate Game is played on a *linear* scale. If you work ten hours, you get ten hours of pay. If you want another ten hours of pay, you need to work another ten hours.

$$10 + 10 = \underline{20}$$

However, in the Leverage Game, players *multiply* their time and effort, not add it up. They use the rules of a new game to increase the outcome of their efforts. Instead of simply adding, they are multiplying. In the Leverage Game, 10 hours of work can pay off with much greater income.

10 x 10 = <u>100</u>

When you learn to play the Leverage Game, you go from time management to *T i m e s* Management. You are learning to multiply your efforts instead of just adding them up. You also learn to use the efforts of others. As a wise businessman once said, "I would rather have 1% of the effort of 100 men than 100% of the effort of one man."

Instead of trading time for dollars, you will learn to trade time for equity. Then you will use that equity

Time Out – Leverage Your Way Out of Debt

A couple from Florida was in financial trouble. Joan and Greg owed over $40,000 in consumer debt, and it was growing each year. A financial planner was working with the couple to help them get control of their lives and get out of debt. What was different about this situation was that the financial planner was not just talking about lowering their expenses; she was also praising the couple for *increasing* their income each month.

By reducing their expenses, the couple was able to "save" $700 per month. They applied that amount to their debt, and had already reduced what they owed to $35,000. But, the amazing thing was that Joan had a business of her own. She was an independent distributor for a company that sold commonly used products.

In one week, Joan had sold enough products to make a $350 profit. The financial planner estimated that it took Joan about five hours to make the sales. Joan's extra work time that week was worth $70 per hour. This rate was considerably higher than what she made on her job!

However, the financial planner failed to point out something very significant. Besides selling the products, Joan also sponsored some people for her business. These new, independent business owners would also be selling products—and sponsoring other business people. How much was Joan's time worth for this part of her business? Suppose she made an extra $100 per month from each of the two people that she sponsored. That would be an extra $2400 per year! How much is her extra time worth now?

Joan created customer equity because her customers are buying common, reusable items. She created network equity because she will have a continuing income from her new business partners. And, as the income from her personal business grows, she will continue to reduce her debt, so she will no longer be using her future time to pay past debts.

to work for you—more work than you could ever do. This equity will continue working day and night, forever. You, on the other hand, will not be working. You will use the time you gain for whatever you want. This is the beauty of the Leverage Game.

Let's take a specific example. If you get paid $25 per hour on your job, then one hour produced $25 in return. If you work 10 hours, then you earn $250.

But suppose you spent those 10 hours creating equity, rather than working on your job. (You will learn a great deal more about the concept of equity in the next chapter.) Now, that equity can go to work for you. It never gets tired. It never needs a day off. It doesn't call in sick. It just keeps producing! You have leveraged your time. You have turned 10 hours of work into many, many hours of return value.

Why Play the Leverage Game?

You should play the Leverage Game because it is the only game you can win. Also, it is the only game that other people can win at the same time. Finally, it is the best way—the *only* way—I know to overcome Time Poverty.

Right now you are playing the wrong game. It isn't your fault. Everyone told you to play the wrong game. It is the way we are raised. Everyone tells you that you are on the right track, going in the right direction. But if you *are* playing the right game, then why don't you have time? Why is tomorrow going to be just as stressful as today? Why are you working so hard for so many years? If this is the right game, shouldn't you be doing better each year, and not worse?

Leveraging your time means increasing outcomes, not inputs. Playing the Leverage Game means getting more out of every hour you spend. And, if you do it right, it means getting more results forever—without more work.

How to Win the Leverage Game

Too many people don't know the rules for the Leverage Game. They think that getting a good education, getting a job and working hard will help them win. They imagine themselves getting promotions at work by working harder than anyone else. They expect that "someday" they will retire and get the opportunity to do all the things they had to put off doing.

Folks, it just doesn't work that way. If you want to win the Leverage Game, if you want to have money and the time to spend it while you are still young enough to enjoy it, if you want to have strong relationships and a fulfilling life, you have to learn some new rules.

Rules of the Leverage Game

The rules are simple. You will learn more about them throughout this book. In fact, by the time you are finished reading, you will be absolutely ready to start applying them. Here is a sample of some of the rules:

1. **Learn to multiply.** Don't think in terms of addition. If you want more, look for ways to get it done by doing less, not more.

2. **Increase the *value* of your time, don't increase your time.** If you can create more without working more, you have automatically made your time more valuable.

3. **Use your time to BUILD, not BUY.** Build equity that does the work for you. You don't want to work forever—but your equity will work forever. Don't spend your money on "stuff" when you can invest it into income-producing assets.

4. **Build a toll booth, not a toil booth.** You aren't interested in working, you are interested in collecting. Find a massive, dynamic trend and take part. Even if you only get a small part of each transaction, it will add up quickly.

5. **Get a mentor, be a mentor.** In the Leverage Game, the object is to develop a network of winners. You will need help, and it is your responsibility to pass that help on to your friends and family.

How Do You Know When You Win?

Winning depends on what your dreams are! When you are living your dreams, you have won. When you have time and money, great relationships and a fulfilling, meaningful life, you have won.

It works like this. You will have two sides to your wealth-producing life: your job and your personal business. When you begin playing the Leverage Game, the two sides will look like this:

As you begin to develop your personal business, the picture may change.

If you apply yourself, and if your dream is strong enough, your position will soon look like this:

Finally, as you invest your profits into equity-producing assets, you will develop a third income-producing area of your life.

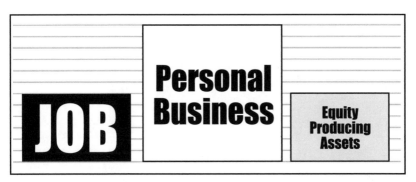

Then, you can reduce, or eliminate, the job portion. This will free up tremendous amounts of time. You are now playing the Leverage Game with real intensity.

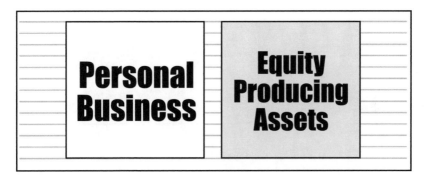

You win! You are now retired from your job, but you are not retired from personal growth, income production, relationships and rewards. In fact, you are living a wealthy life that your friends, those who are still playing the Corporate Game, will never achieve.

That is how you play, and win, the Leverage Game!

Part 2

How to Create a Time-Rich Life

Part 2:

How to Create a Time-Rich Life

Okay, now you know the problem. You have been playing the wrong game, trying to balance your life at too low a lifestyle level, trading your time away for dollars, and missing the opportunity to multiply your efforts for far greater rewards. Are you ready to change all that?

In Part 2, *How to Create a Time-Rich Life*, you will get step-by-step instructions for achieving a Time-Rich lifestyle. You will have the tools you need to win back your time and create wealth.

You will learn the value of equity—and how to use it to replace your work hours with powerful, wealth building results. And, you will see how the Time-Rich use simple techniques to increase the value of each and every waking hour. Are you reaching your full potential? Is your time undervalued? How much SHOULD your time be worth?

The five steps to a Time-Rich lifestyle will set you free—free to spend your time the way you like, free to teach your children how to avoid losing time games, free from worry about mortgage payments, Social Security and "living on a fixed income."

Best of all, you will learn how to set, visualize and fulfill your dreams. Remember, many people are already living at a high lifestyle level. You aren't breaking new ground; you are just joining a different crowd.

It doesn't matter who you are, how young or how old. The time is now!

Chapter 7

The Ecstasy of Equity

Carpe per diem. Seize the check.

— Robin Williams

I remember sitting in my Freshman Accounting class and learning about owner's equity. "When you construct a balance sheet," said Professor Fisher, "you put the assets on one side and the liabilities on the other. If you have more assets than liabilities, you have equity. Equity is good!"

Now, while I understood the *concept* of equity, I really didn't understand the full power of the word. I didn't understand that the true sign of a solid business is that you own more than you owe. In those days, I was more concerned about income. I was setting my sights on making money, not on keeping that money.

In his blockbuster book *Rich Dad, Poor Dad*, Robert Kiyosaki explains it very well. He says that the rich understand how to keep their money. The poor only understand how to work for money. The poor pay taxes, high taxes, on every cent they make. The rich pay taxes—but at a much lower rate—because they make money a different way. The rich create *capital gains*, while the poor create a *paycheck*.

Who do you think has more control of their time? Do you think a person who works hard, trading hour after hour of their time for dollars, then pays high taxes on those dollars has more time? Or, do you think the person who puts their money to work, then pays less taxes on capital gains, has more time? You know which one is better off, don't you?

Work or Worth?

Most people would like to be millionaires. Yet very few people actually understand what it means to be a millionaire. Does it mean you earn a million dollars per year? Does it mean you are actually worth more than $1,000,000?

Being a millionaire means that you own $1 million of something. It means that, on your balance sheet, your assets are worth $1 million more than your liabilities. It means that you own $1 million more than you owe!

If a person has $50 million worth of assets in, say, real estate, but he owes the bank $49.5 million in mortgages, he is not a millionaire. He is only a half-millionaire.

A millionaire is someone who actually owns something worth a million dollars—and doesn't owe any money on it. A millionaire is not a lifestyle, it is a bank statement.

In their great book *The Millionaire Next Door*, authors Thomas J. Stanley and William D. Danko describe the typical American millionaire. They talk about a person who drives a Buick, not a Mercedes. They talk about someone who may live in a rather modest house. They describe someone who has saved their money, not spent it. But, they also contrast real millionaires with people who don't have the assets, but live a millionaire's *lifestyle*.

When I talk to you about creating equity, I am talking about becoming a millionaire, with money or assets that are worth more than $1 million. I am talking about establishing *equity* that delivers powerful, life altering income forever. And I am talking about using the equity-produced income to create time—lots and lots of time!

How Does Equity Create Time?

Here is how most people spend their lives:

They get a job and buy some stuff. Some of the stuff, like cars, they buy *on time*, which is to say, they take out a loan that must be paid back *over time*. Then they get a promotion, and buy a better car, thus "using up" the promotion in monthly payments. They get another promotion, and they buy a bigger house. The increased mortgage "uses up" the increase in their pay. They are working harder and harder, trying to get promotion after promotion. But, every time they get a promotion, they spend the extra money on something that costs that much money. They trade more and more time for more and more money, so they can buy more and more stuff on time.

According to *Rich Dad, Poor Dad* author Kiyosaki, most people are spending their money on liabilities, not on assets. They have locked themselves into a vicious cycle of trading time for dollars, and dollars for stuff. They have great income — but they are spending all of their time to get it. And, they are spending all of their income on stuff that is not worth one half of what they paid for it one year later.

If you buy a new car for $30,000, how much is it worth the day after you drive it off the lot? Is it worth $30,000? Is it worth $35,000? No, it has depreciated! It is worth less than you paid for it yesterday! If you had to trade it in, if you had to sell it, you would not get more than 90% of what you paid for it. You lost equity!

If your payments on that car are $450 per month, would you have to pay less because your car is worth less? No! You pay the same amount, month after month, no matter how little the car is worth.

You have lost equity. In fact, when you buy something on time, you are losing equity at an alarming rate. If you paid $30,000 for the car, but you pay for it over time, you may pay close to $40,000 over five years. But, what is that $30,000 car worth on the last day of your payments? It is worth about $15,000. You are losing money fast!

The problem is that if you are like most people, you make your money for that car payment by trading your time. So, you trade hour after hour for money that is worth less and less. It is no wonder that you are running out of time. You can't work fast enough, or long enough, or efficiently enough, to overcome this terrible equation. You are trapped on the Fast Track, along with almost everyone else.

To overcome this problem you need to build equity. After all, you only have so much time in a day, a week, or a year. You can spend your time working for money, or spend your time building assets and equity. Then, these equities produce income, and you can go fishing.

Build Equity, Build Time

Suppose you get off the Fast Track—not just at work, but with your purchasing habits as well. Suppose you stop buying things that lose money and start buying things that make money.

You need to invest your money in assets that actually produce income, instead of losing money. That is a winning formula. That is the kind of thinking that will make it possible for you to have time in your life, because you won't be locked into the constant earn and spend, earn and spend rat race that has trapped you in a Time-Poor lifestyle for so long.

Imagine these scenarios:

You buy a car with a five-year loan. After five years, you pay off the car, keep it, and use the payment money to invest in EQUITY. Instead of buying a new car, you put the payments ($450 per month) into the mortgage of an investment property. You'd be building equity with each mortgage payment. Or, you could invest that $450 per month into a business. Would that make a difference? Of course it would. You would have equity, not a liability!

Most people spend their entire lives spending money on things that cost them time—by tying them to a job that requires time to make the payments, instead of investing that money into assets that actually produce income. What if you spent a lifetime buying assets that produced income? Would you eventually have enough income to retire? Could you turn down the overtime because you have a steady, dependable, risk-free income source outside your job? Would you have more time if your money came from a source that did not require you to spend time to get the money?

Let's look at the equity position of an average family. Here is a typical balance sheet:

Assets:	
Home (estimated value)	300,000
Cars	
His	18,000
Hers	15,000
401 (k)	70,000
Furniture, etc.	21,000
Life Insurance cash value	7,300
Stocks, bonds, and mutual funds	10,000
Bank Accounts	6,000
Total	**447,300**
Liabilities:	
Mortgage	213,400
Home Equity Loan	40,000
Car Loans	
His	10,000
Hers	11,000
Credit cards	6,000
Student loans	15,000
Furniture loans	5,000
Orthodontist	3,000
Total	**303,400**

This family has a small net worth. Their total assets minus their total liabilities is $143,900. They have very little equity. Yes, they have a relatively nice lifestyle. They have a comfortable home, a big screen TV, and two cars. Their home is nicely furnished. They take a vacation each year, pay their bills on time and watch what they spend.

However, they both work long hours to keep up their lifestyle. And, because they are not developing any assets that will produce income, they will never, never be able to stop working so hard. In a few years, they will both need a new car, which will increase and prolong their car payments. The kids will need money for school—even a state college is getting expensive. Right now, they are all in good health, but what will happen if something goes wrong?

This couple has another twenty years until retirement, so they hope to build their retirement savings. However, they do not have a specific goal. Will they be able to live on what they save?

They have equity in their home. And, their neighborhood is appreciating well. But, can they USE that money? Yes, they can take a home equity loan to pay for things like college, but that all has to be paid back! And, it raises their monthly payments, making it necessary for them to work even harder to get promotions to pay for the new loans.

This couple is in their 40's. They each have a college degree, and they have each been working for over twenty years. They will each work for *another* twenty years, then take low-paying "retirement" jobs to keep some money coming in.

After a combined total of **FORTY YEARS OF WORK**, wouldn't it be nice if they were worth more than $143,900? What will they be worth in another twenty years? Will they EVER have enough money and income to stop working so hard? Will they ever have the time to do the things they want in life? And, if they do have that time, will they have the money to enjoy it?

What happens if something goes wrong? What if one of the kids develops an illness that requires attention? What if one of the parents has a disability? What if one of them gets laid off and it takes a while for them to find another job? Will the new job pay as much?

And, this is the absolute worst question I have to ask you: *What happens if everything goes exactly right? Even if everything goes according to their plan, they will never have much money, they will never have much time, and they will teach their children to do the same thing, for another forty or fifty years!* What is the answer to their problem? They need to build income-producing equity.

How to Build Equity: Investment Properties

There are two ways to make money with investment properties. One is to buy homes and rent them out. This method produces both equity and income. Your income is the difference between what your renters pay you and what you pay to keep the property. You build equity by paying off the mortgage. If you do it right, you are paying off the mortgage with the *renter's* money!

In this book we talk about developing ways to generate income, without trading time for dollars. And, we talk about creating equity that will produce more income. If your renters pay for your mortgage, and if they provide you with income, they are trading their time for dollars, and you are not.

Time Out – Time Debt

All debt is time debt. If you hope to overcome Time Poverty, this is a concept that you need to understand.

Any form of debt places a burden on your time. When you owe something to someone else, you are, in a sense, working for them. You can't take time off. You can't decide whether or not you will work. You OWE that person and you must pay them back.

Credit card debt is an excellent example of time debt. Almost nothing you buy with a credit card is an asset. Almost everything you buy is a liability or an expense. If you purchase a dinner with a credit card, you owe the bank the money for that dinner. Now, the next time you go to work, you are working for the bank. You are not working for yourself.

If you trade your time for dollars on a job, you are not borrowing money when you use a credit card; you are borrowing on your future time. The more you borrow, the more you owe. The more you owe, the longer you have to work to pay it off!

Do you wonder where your time went? It went to all the people that lent you money. It went to credit card companies, banks, car companies, furniture companies, etc. Every time you buy something "on time" you are buying it on YOUR time, not THEIR time.

Banks and other lenders are smart. They use your time to make their money. Maybe you should get smart. Start using assets to produce income. Stop trading your time for dollars, and start using dollars to generate time.

with income, they are trading their time for dollars, and you are not.

The second way to make money in real estate is through appreciation. In a good market, the value of your house increases, giving you more equity. You can sell the house later and take the money, or you can borrow on that equity to buy more houses or other assets.

How to Build Equity: Retirement Accounts

Jeanne and I do not take the time to invest in individual stocks in the stock market. We don't have the patience to analyze stocks and follow the trends. Some people enjoy this, and they don't mind putting in the time to watch their investments. We invest our money in mutual funds, especially through my retirement accounts.

There are several advantages. First, the earnings are tax-deferred. That is, we will not pay any tax on them until we actually withdraw the funds. Second, the university where I work puts money into my retirement account for me. If your employer has a "matching" policy for your retirement account, make sure that you take advantage of it. This is like free money. Third, we do not have to manage the money. Someone else, who knows more about that stuff than I do, does it for me.

I am not an expert on investing, but I do know this: You need to look at the long term when investing, and, you need to diversify your money. Don't put it all into one stock, or one type of investment. If your company invests your retirement plan exclusively into their own stock, watch out!

However, over the long term, by investing your money into tax-deferred, diversified accounts, and by taking advantage of your company's retirement plan (or SEP or IRA if you are self-employed) you can create a nice income for later in life. And, in some cases, such as to pay for college tuition for your kids, you can withdraw the money early without penalty.

How to Build Equity: Personal Businesses

Creating a personal business is a perfect way for ordinary men and women to create income-producing, time-leveraging equity. It is the very best way to overcome Time Poverty because it creates equity (something of value that you own) and income (continuous streams of cash). By investing a little time and

money in the right kind of personal business, you can create leverage.

When you leverage your time through a personal business, you gain power, without expending time and money. You use someone else's time and money!

Here are two ways to leverage your time and money in a personal business to create equity.

- Don't reinvent the wheel! Join a business system. Look for a business where people like you are successful. They have already learned how to make a profit. Follow the rules, suggestions and leadership of the successful people in your business. Read their books, listen to their CD's, and so forth. This will give you business equity that is worth far more than the time and money you invest.

- Build a customer base. Did you know that big businesses, I mean BIG companies, think of their customers as an asset? They call it customer equity. If you can develop loyal customers, or if you can develop loyal members in your personal business, this creates income-producing equity. It costs you very little, and it can make you a fortune—or a lifestyle!

Building a personal business is such an important part of overcoming Time Poverty that I've devoted the next chapter to it.

How to Build Equity: Paying Off Liabilities

No discussion of equity creation would be complete without mentioning strategies for reducing liabilities. Any time you reduce your liabilities by one dollar, you automatically increase your equity by one dollar. If you pay $100 off your house mortgage, you add $100 to your net worth.

You can create equity by paying off your bills and loans. Pay off those credit cards, pay off those auto loans. You should not be borrowing money to buy things that do not produce income. Instead, save the money in an interest bearing account until you have enough to pay cash!

I would never discourage people from paying off their liabilities. But, most people do not have income-producing assets. So, while paying off $5,000 in credit card debt does, technically, increase your net worth by $5,000, it does not produce any income. It only reduces debt.

So, your debt *reducing* strategy is not complete unless it is coupled with an income *increasing* strategy. When you pay off a car, credit card or other debt, you eliminate a monthly payment. Now, use that monthly payment to buy an income-producing asset.

The Five Kinds of Equity

Here are five types of equity you can create:

1. **Customer Equity**—Create loyal customers in your personal business. It takes some time to get their first order, but the RE-ORDER doesn't take any time at all! And, you make just as much money from the re-orders.

2. **System Equity**—When you pay a small fee to create a personal business with an existing company, you get all their SYSTEMS! This is like putting money in your pocket. You get marketing, training, product development and more. You make money by letting them work for you to create promotional material, accept payments, pay dividends, etc.

3. **Network Equity**—If your personal business has a multi-level payout, you make money when other people on your team make money. This is an incredible equity position. You can multiply the results of your work by showing others how to achieve personal success.

4. **Asset Equity**—Use the profits from your business to purchase income-producing assets. This is a great strategy for diversifying your position.

5. **Mentor Equity**—Almost no one understands the power of this equity. In a traditional job, you are "kicked out the door" when you retire. If you have the right kind of personal business, you GAIN equity when you retire. You can share your knowledge with others. They will pay you for your experience. They want to keep you around, not throw you out. Mentor equity produces money, but it gives you an additional bonus—a meaningful, involved and rewarding retirement. Best of all, you can use Mentor Equity at any age!

Use Equity to Build Income

Ultimately, you want to overcome Time Poverty. Creating massive, income-producing equity is an important key. You can then use the income and capital gains the equity produces to buy back some of your time.

Use equity to produce residual income that keeps coming in, even after you stop working for it. Imagine an income stream that is quite separate from your job. Imagine a huge net worth that can be turned into cash if necessary. Imagine the reduction in stress when you have a solid, dependable financial position.

Imagine yourself with time, because now you do not have to trade that time for dollars!

Chapter 8

A Business of Your Own

> *Going into business for yourself, becoming
> an entrepreneur, is the modern-day
> equivalent of pioneering on the old frontier.*
>
> — Louis E. Boone

There are many advantages to owning a personal business. You get an opportunity to create wealth, meet new people, mentor others, and take advantage of tax benefits. And, while all of these things are great, I believe the best advantage to owning a personal business is that you learn how to create equity by working with people. These people may be your customers, your partners, your mentors, or your friends. Owning a personal business is a great way to start trading time for equity.

I Haven't Got Time For That!

You are probably saying, "But wait, I am already short of time. How can I start a personal business right now? It takes time and money to start a personal business. I thought time and money were what I would *get*, not *give up!*"

Hang in there: I *am* going to ask you to spend some time and money right now, so that you can have much *more* time and money later. It will take some effort, and it will be tough for a while, but that is the price you must pay to have choices.

The Personal Business Choice

The first step to choosing a personal business is to review the kinds of businesses that ordinary people can start. You want one that allows you the freedom to do as much or as little as you like—without penalty. You want a business that is there for you when you have time, and not one that requires constant attention.

Today, *everyone* should be able to find a personal business that fits their needs. However, most personal businesses can be divided into two categories:

1. YOYO (You're On Your Own)—This term covers a whole range of businesses, from trading on eBay, to hobby-related businesses, to flea markets, to real estate. A YOYO might be a great way to get started.

2. POPPER (Plenty of Partners Producing Enormous Rewards)—These are businesses that are set up already and involve other people. They range from direct selling businesses, such as gift baskets, cosmetics, or other consumer goods, to networking businesses, which are multi-level distribution companies.

In either case, whether you operate a YOYO or a POPPER, you are in business for yourself. You will learn important lessons about customers, budgeting, sales and follow-up. And, you can apply those lessons to your current job to become a better employee.

Today, too many people are lost in the layers of corporate obscurity. Most people never even see a customer, let alone deal with one. Far too many employees are unaware of the principles of business—finding a product that people need, looking for people with a problem, and then solving that problem in a profitable way. The experience of actually owning and operating your own business is a powerful lesson.

Are You a YOYO or a POPPER?

So, what kind of business should you start? The answer depends on your goals.

A **YOYO** business is easy to start. Do something you enjoy. For example, if you like to fish, maybe you can learn to repair fishing rods and reels. There are even some courses you can buy that will teach you how to do it. (If you do start this type of business, please let me know, as I have several rods and reels that need to be fixed!)

An easy way to start a YOYO business is to start trading on eBay. Look around your house. Do you have anything that is unusual, or rare, or just plain strange? Or, do you have "extras" of something? How about expertise or knowledge that others can use?

Here are two examples of people who started a YOYO business on eBay.

One of my students is from Japan. He has read all of my books and he believes in the free enterprise system. Last year, he found some great ties at a store near our university in Miami. The ties were far less expen-

Time Out – Work for Yourself

I am not saying you shouldn't have a job. I am saying you shouldn't think like you are working for someone else. You should always *think* like you are working for yourself and your family. There is a big difference.

I am a professor at Florida International University in Miami. But it is still a job. I still have a boss and he still has strange ideas about how I should live my life and spend my time. After all, he is a boss.

I don't think of myself as an employee of FIU. I work for myself and I am simply contracting my services to FIU. I give them a great exchange for their money. They get outstanding teaching, fantastic research and writing, and a wonderful colleague. It is a great bargain for them.

Because I do not consider myself their employee, I keep myself ready for any opportunity that comes along. While others are trading away their free time in an effort to earn a few extra dollars or get a promotion, I am thinking of ways to *leverage* my time and money to create a fantastic lifestyle.

Is this a small point, a small difference? No, it is a *huge* difference. My attitude is simple. I work for myself and my family. We are the bosses. We know what we want and only we can decide how to spend my time.

I love my job, but I love my life a lot more.

sive here than in Japan. He put an ad on eBay, took orders, bought the ties, shipped them to Japan and made a profit. Then, he did it again, and again, and again! Pretty soon, his dorm room was full of ties, and he was going to the post office every day. He has now expanded his line to include other types of clothing.

Here's another example. One of my relatives is great at restoring old cars. When he was younger he had a Fiat Spider automobile that he really loved. Now, in his 50s, he spent two years rebuilding one. He video-taped the process and will soon release a "make-over manual" for car buffs. He plans to sell the video/book series on eBay.

Other friends have worked YOYO businesses as well. One couple bought children's books and sold them at flea markets. They did quite well. Several people sold their crafts at shows and festivals. When I was young, my mother used to be quite an accomplished painter. She exhibited and sold her art in stores near our Philadelphia home.

YOYO's have their good points. They are easy to start. Most people do things that interest them. YOYO's are often a great way to pick up some fast cash. They can also be great opportunities to involve the entire family. Get the kids involved and spend some time together. I can still remember watching my Mom paint, then going to the stores with her to collect the money from her sales.

On the other hand, as the name YOYO implies, you really are on your own. There is no one to show you how to set up your business. No one else benefits from what you do, so there is no reason for them to help you. YOYO's can be very time-consuming as well. My student spends a great deal of time shopping, taking orders, packaging clothing and shipping it.

So how does a **POPPER** work? POPPERS involve people in the *distribution* of existing products in an organized business. Generally, POPPERS, whether they are direct selling companies or network marketing companies, have training programs, support systems and promotional materials. Here are a few examples:

Party Companies—While these companies have been around for a long time, they have gained popularity in recent years. Generally, a business owner invites friends, relatives and acquaintances to a "party" where products are displayed and can be purchased. And, in most companies, business owners can recruit other people to hold more parties, thus leveraging income.

Direct Sales— These companies are based on a long tradition of face-to-face selling. However, today, many of them utilize electronic techniques to enhance the selling possibilities. Again, these are well established companies who use a sales force of personal business owners. Instead of being an employee, the sales people actually own their companies.

Network Marketing—These companies use a unique system of distribution to move products and services to their customers. Individual business owners buy products for personal use and also sell products to customers. They can make money, just like direct sellers, but networkers have an added profit opportunity. They can recruit others to do the same

---

Time Out – The 80/20 Rule

If you want to make the most of your time, learn the 80/20 rule. It was developed in the early part of the twentieth century by a man named Wifredo Pareto. In fact, it is sometimes called the Pareto Principle.

Pareto found that 80% of the results come from 20% of the causes. This applies to both the positive and negative aspects of life. For example, while 20% of your customers produce 80% of the sales, 80% of the problems come from only 20% of the people!

In order to maximize your time, you need to find the right 20% and put 80% of your efforts to work. This will leverage your results dramatically.

Use the Pareto Principle in your personal business in connection with the A, B, C's of selling. Customize for A relationships and standardize for C relationships. When you standardize, use tapes, computer files, web sites and other "static" documents that answer questions and solve simple problems. 80% of the problems can be solved this way.

However, when you find an A person or product, you want to specialize in that area. You want to put effort into that situation. You will do whatever it takes to solve problems there, because the returns are so high. You are maximizing your effort—and the return on your invested time.

thing, help train them, support them, and earn profits and bonuses based on the volume that moves through their "network" or system.

What do all these POPPERS have in common? They are networks of independent business people who are helping established manufacturers get their products into the hands of consumers.

What are the benefits of being a POPPER? Most POPPERS deal with established businesses and brands. They have quality products that everyone needs. And it is not necessary to hold inventory, bill customers, do accounting, and so forth. These companies handle all that for the individual business owner.

In addition, the profit potential is usually unlimited. This is especially true for companies with a network component. You are not depending on the work of one person when you create a network. Instead, you make money by helping other people make money.

Network companies, as the name implies, provide a terrific opportunity to make new friends and form strong relationships. You can "retire" and still be a viable, valuable part of the system.

Most importantly, a networking company gives you the best opportunity to establish equity! Income-producing equity will give you the free time you want and the money to enjoy it.

To Sum It Up

Today, there is no excuse for not owning a business. The entire tax structure of our country is set up to reward personal businesses. You get to make more money and, more importantly, you get to KEEP more money.

As a personal business owner, you will learn the value of building relationships, how to work with others, the secrets for creating profits and the possibilities of solving people's problems. While this will make you more money, it will also make you more valuable on your present job. You will be more secure, and happier, with your new knowledge.

Finally, be sure to choose the right business for you. Are you looking for a fast profit? Then you might start off with a YOYO. However, if you are looking for a life changing business, if you want unlimited profit potential, if you want support from a well established company and people who want you to succeed, then get into a POPPER!

Chapter 9

The Value of Your Time

> Lost, yesterday, somewhere between Sunrise
> and Sunset, two golden hours, each set with
> sixty diamond minutes. No reward is
> offered, for they are gone forever.
>
> — Horace Mann

Spending Time

I visited a friend of mine who was losing money on his pig farm. My friend had the biggest, fattest pigs in the county, but he still couldn't show a profit. He asked me to come out to the farm and look over the operation.

I arrived on a beautiful Saturday afternoon. My friend was just returning to the barn CARRYING a huge, fat pig in his arms. He put the pig into a stall, then, wiping off his hands, he walked over to me.

"That was sure a big pig," I said. "Are they all that large?"

"Every one of them," he replied. "And I have dozens."

"What's your secret?" I asked.

He pointed. "Do you see that big apple orchard over there? Each morning, I come out to the barn, pick up one pig, carry him out to that orchard and hold him up while he eats an apple."

"What happens when he finishes the apple?" I asked.

"Well, I sort of move around the apple tree a little bit until he finds another one. Then I let him eat that one too. I keep doing it until he is full, and then I carry him back to the barn and get another pig."

"You do that with each and every pig, each and every day?" I asked.

"Sure do," he said. "That's how they get so fat. That's my secret!"

I was stunned. "Doesn't that take a lot of time?"

"So what?" he said. "What's time to a pig?"

That farmer was confused. In his mind, he was in the business of creating fat pigs. He didn't care how much time it took him. The truth is, he didn't place any value on his own time. He spent all his time carrying pigs rather than figuring out ways to make his business profitable. As long as he did the work, he thought he was doing the right thing.

How many people do you know who think as long as they are busy, they are doing the right thing? They are confused about what their *real* mission is.

The same is true of how so many people view their jobs. They will find things to do to fill in the workdays, and then they will stay *overtime* so that they get a real feeling of being busy.

In almost any task, it is not the work; it is the *result* that counts. People who have a high value on their time know that their time is valuable because it is limited. Don't just do work, do the things that produce results. And make sure that those results will meet your goals and dreams.

Think of *your* time, not your boss's time, or your customer's time. You are in control of your time. You must select the activities that produce results. Otherwise, you will be asking yourself, "Hey, what's time to a pig?"

How Much is Your Time Worth?

An important step in overcoming Time Poverty is to calculate the exact value of your time. Most people have absolutely no idea how much their time is worth per hour. Yet this simple calculation is extremely important in creating more valuable time. You have to know where you are now in order to move on.

We are going to make an assumption here. We are going to assume that your time is worth what you are currently being paid for it. Is that fair? After all, if your time was worth more, you would get paid more, right? If it was worth less, you would get paid less.

Calculate Your Time Value

This is a simple calculation. You only need to know two things:

1. How much you make per year.
2. How many hours per week you spend working for that money.

Let's take an example. A man earns $50,000 per year and works 40 hours per week on average. We would calculate the value of his time as follows:

$50,000 divided by 50 weeks = $1,000 per week

(I know there are actually 52 weeks per year, but it is much easier to divide by 50 — and this is only an estimate!)

$1,000 per week divided by 40 hours per week = $25 per hour.

This man's time is worth $25 per hour. It MUST be worth $25 per hour. If it were worth less, he would be paid less. *If it were worth more, he would be making more money for the same amount of work.*

A New Millennium Promotion

Let's say that the man is on salary, and he gets a "new millennium promotion." What is a new millennium promotion? There are two types.

The first kind is when other people are getting laid off and your boss says, "You are not getting laid off! Congratulations!" The problem is, you don't get any more money per hour, and you end up doing some of the work that the people who just got laid off used to do. This means that you are working more hours per week for the same money. Instead of being worth $25 per hour, your time is now only worth $20 per hour because you still make $50,000 and are now working 50 hours per week!

The second type of new millennium promotion is when you actually do get a promotion, but you still have to do all the things you *were* doing—with additional responsibilities. I know one guy who was joking about his company. "The truth is," he said, "when you get a promotion, you keep your old job *and* do the new one, because they don't hire anyone new to do your old job!" Like the first new millennium promotion, you're probably working more hours per week for the same money.

A Calculation Shortcut

In his great book, *Success Is Not An Accident*, Tommy Newberry uses a grid to make calculating the value of your time much quicker and easier. Look at this grid:

Hours per week

	30	40	50	60
25	17	13	10	8
50	33	25	20	17
75	50	37	30	25
100	67	50	40	33
150	100	75	60	50
300	200	150	120	100
500	333	250	200	167

Annual Salary in Thousands

On the left side of the grid you will find annual earnings. It starts at $25K and goes up to $500K. Across the top are hours worked per week. They start at 30 and go up to 60. To calculate the value of your time using the grid, just find your annual earnings in the first column and go across the row until it intercepts the column under the amount of hours you work per week.

For example, if you earn $50,000 per year, find that number in the first column. If you work 40 hours per week, move across the $50,000 row until you find the column under 40 hours. That number is $25, just like in the earlier example. If you work 50 hours per week for your $50,000, then your time is worth $20 per hour.

The Problem For Most People

When most people want to make more money, they try to do it by moving across the time row, instead of moving down the earnings column. We are trained by our schools, bosses, family and friends to think of ourselves as being worth a certain amount. So, we naturally try to solve our money problems by spending more time EARNING money. Instead, we should make our time more valuable—each and every hour—so that we can spend the same amount of time, or even better, less time making more money. The only way to do this is to make our time more valuable!

The Work You Are About To Do?

Consider this situation:

You have been on your job for about two years. You like your job, but it is hard to get excited about it sometimes. In fact, your sales have started to slip.

One day your boss walks into your office and says she needs to meet with you.

Time Out – Vacations

According to *Newsweek*, Americans lost 415,000,000 vacation days last year because they were just too busy to take them! That is three days for every single worker in the United States. Many companies have instituted a "use it or lose it" policy. If you don't take your time off in a given calendar year, you can't use it in the following years. Even if companies did not have such a policy, it is unlikely that people who are too busy to take their earned vacation this year can take more of it next year.

The *Newsweek* writers suggest three tactics to make use of those vacation days:

1. Take "border days" at the beginning and end of each business trip. Going to a nice place for a meeting? Why not arrive a day early and stay a day later?

2. Ask for three hours off each Friday afternoon or Monday morning.

3. Take a single vacation day on Wednesday and go to the spa.

What do I suggest? Get a better life! If you haven't got time to take your vacation then you better keep reading this book!

"We have been reviewing the performances of all our people and we see that you have not been doing all that well," she says. "Your customers can't find you when they call. The other employees say that you are asleep in many of the meetings. What is going on?"

You reply, "Well, I know I haven't been my best. But, I think I can do better. How about if we meet a year from now and we review my performance? I know you will be happier because I will learn how to do my job better. By next year, I will be the great employee you always wanted."

"That will be great," says your boss. "A year from now, I know you will be wonderful. Let's give you a raise now, so that as you get better, you will be paid properly."

Has this ever happened? Of course not. Your boss isn't going to give you a raise for work you are about to do. You only get a raise when you have shown you can do the extra work.

No one ever gives you a raise for work you are about to do. And you cannot give yourself a raise for work you are about to do.

Your boss is only going to give you a raise if you demonstrate that you are capable of operating at a higher level. And, in your own business, no one is going to give you money for promising to perform some task. You actually have to do the work. Then, and only then, do you get the money.

Increasing the Value of Your Time

So, you will not get a raise for work you are about to do. This applies directly to the problem of how to make your time more valuable. *You have to **act** like your time is worth more in order for it to actually be worth more.*

Let's use a specific example so you can really understand clearly.

Lisa makes $50,000 per year and works 40 hours per week. Her time is worth $25 per hour. She wants to make $100,000 per year while still working 40 hours per week. In order to do this, her time must be worth $50 per hour, or *twice* what it is worth now.

Here is the big point: If Lisa wants her time to be worth $50 per hour, then she has to act like her time is worth $50 per hour! In other words, she can't wait until her time is actually worth $50 per hour to start acting like it. *She has to do the work first, then she will get the raise—or give it to herself.*

Where Most People Get Stuck

Too many people think, "My time is worth $25 per hour, so I will *act* like my time is worth $25 per hour. When my time gets to be worth $50 per hour, then I will act like it is worth $50 per hour."

The problem is if you act like your time is only worth $25 per hour, *it will never be worth more.* Remember that no one ever gets paid for work they are about to do. You only get paid for work you have already done. *You have to do the work of someone who is worth more in order to be worth more.*

I talk to so many people who really want to move on financially. They want to overcome their Time Poverty. They want to have security and freedom. They want to make a difference in their lives that will affect the financial and time lifestyles of their children and grandchildren. Yet they are unable to do it because they don't change their basic performance. They *think* like a person who is worth far less than the person they need to become. As a result of this thinking, they stay at their present level and wonder why the world is passing them by.

How $200-an-hour People Think

A friend of mine is a successful business owner. He has a nice home, a great family, and plenty of time to spend with his family.

His son's school was having a fund-raiser. A local stadium donated a concession stand to charities, schools, and other groups to help them raise money. The deal was simple. The group that wanted to raise money supplied eight people to work the concession for two nights. At the end of those two nights, the charity would receive a substantial check, depending on how much they sold.

My friend agreed to work at the stadium, along with seven other fathers. They worked six hours on Friday and another six on Saturday. At the end of the weekend, they had raised around $2,000 for the school.

The school was thrilled, and so were some of the fathers. Their sons were also pleased. After all, their dads had spent "quality time" working for the school. Isn't that what fathers are supposed to do?

My friend wasn't happy at all. He did the following calculations:

8 men times 6 hours on Friday	=	48 hours
8 men times 6 hours on Saturday	=	48 hours
Total		96 hours

He rounded the 96 hours off to 100 hours to allow for planning time, drive time, and so forth. $2,000 divided by 100 hours = $20 per hour!

My friend, owner of a valuable business, gave up 12 hours of his time, away from his family, in order to work for $20 per hour for his son's school! His 12 hours of hard work produced $240 for the school. His conclusion:

"Next year, just ask me for a check! I will spend the time with my family."

Would you have thought like my friend? You would if you treated your time as if it were worth much more than $20 per hour! If you were acting like your time was only worth $10 per hour, this would never occur to you.

I want you to decide how much your time must be worth in order to have the things you want. Then act like your time is worth that much! It is the only way you will ever get more than you have now.

Chapter 10

You *Are* Worth More

The bad news is time flies. The good news is you're the pilot.

— Michael Altshuler

One of my favorite television commercials goes something like this:

A man is his early forties is standing in the front yard of his suburban luxury home. He says, "Do you like my house? It has five bedrooms. I also have two fancy cars and a membership in a very exclusive country club."

As he says this, the home, the cars, and the country club appear on the screen. The impression we get is that this guy is very wealthy.

"How did I get these things?" the man asks. "I am in debt up to my eyeballs!"

This is a classic example of a guy who looks like a millionaire, but who is actually just a step away from being broke and losing it all.

Folks, when I tell you to ACT like your time is worth more, I am not telling you to LIVE like your time is worth more than it actually is.

So many people today live beyond their means. They spend more than they have or can ever pay back. The average family in America today has over $8,000 in credit card debt. This is only *credit card* debt, and doesn't count car loans, mortgages, school loans, and so forth. In fact, the average family is swimming—if not drowning—in debt.

How many people do you know who buy things on credit? They want those things, and they think they deserve those things. *They want to **look** like they deserve those things.* So many people listen to advice—great advice—then twist it to fit their own actions, even when those actions could not possibly support their lifestyle.

That is why I say, "*Act* like your time is worth more than it is, but don't *live* like your time is worth more than it is."

Planning the Future versus Fixing the Past

Do you want to spend your time planning for a better future, then acting on that plan, or do you want to spend all your life trying to recover from mistakes? People who act on their plans for the future will have a much better chance for success than those who try to catch up from past mistakes. They will pass on valuable lessons to their kids, have less stress, and have a better lifestyle overall.

Let's take two hypothetical couples. I will show you what I mean.

Joe and his wife live in a decent neighborhood. They have two cars and two jobs. Their combined incomes are $80,000 per year.

Frank and his wife live in the same neighborhood. They also make $80,000 per year.

Each couple has two small children. They want their kids to go to a nice school. That may mean moving to a different neighborhood where the schools are better. They also want to spend time with their kids. They take a nice vacation each year. In other words, they are very much alike in what they WANT out of life.

But each couple takes a radically different approach to their financial lives.

Frank and his wife decide that there is no time like the present to get a new home in a better school district. They get a mortgage and move. In the new neighborhood, everyone drives nice cars, and Frank wants to fit in. He and his wife each get a new car. He gets a sporty SAV (suburban assault vehicle) and she gets the latest minivan. They take a vacation at the same resort as some of the other neighbors. Of course, they put it all on their credit cards—with the intentions of paying it off later.

Now, Frank and his wife are in a trap. They are living like they want, but their incomes are not sufficient to support it. Frank and his wife are good communicators though, so they talk about what to do.

"I can get some overtime at work," Frank says. "My boss is always asking for volunteers to put in an extra shift on Saturday and Sunday."

"I can do some things too," says his wife. "If you are not going to be home on the weekends, I might as well pick up an extra shift on Saturdays. My sister will watch the kids for us if we can watch hers during the week."

While this couple is showing great teamwork, they are missing the point. They wanted to move to the new neighborhood to give their family a better lifestyle. What kind of lifestyle will they have now? Frank and his wife will be working long hours and their kids will be with their aunt! As long as they try to make more money by spending more time doing it, they will never have a better lifestyle.

On the other hand, Joe and his wife also want a better lifestyle. They estimate that they will need about another $20,000 per year in order to make the move to a better neighborhood. Currently, Joe makes $50,000 per year and his wife makes $30,000. Besides the additional $20,000, they want one of them to stay home with the kids full time. Since his wife is making less, Joe knows that it is more logical to replace her income than his.

Now, the couple has a solid goal. They need an additional $50,000 per year in order to reach their dreams. They don't want to work more hours. In fact, they want to work less! Therefore, *they must make each work hour more valuable in order to reach their goals.*

How do they do it? First of all, they protect their current sources of income. Joe's wife is willing to go to work for another year. She does a great job to protect that income. Joe does the same thing. It is even more important for him now. He becomes a much better employee so that there will be no problem with his primary source of income.

But the couple begins to consider other possibilities. They start to look for opportunities. They develop time-value

---

Time Out - Develop Anticipation, Not Anxiety

You have a lot of work to do. After all, you have to make some big changes in your life. Will you focus on the work—and all the challenges of doing something new—or will you set your sights on your dream? In the first case, you are working with anxiety, in the second, anticipation.

Anxiety is stress. It is worrying about something in the future. I once heard someone say that anxiety is "paying for a debt you haven't incurred yet." You are anxious about something that is about to happen, and you don't even know if it WILL happen! Don't worry so much.

For example, if you want to start your own business, but you are so worried about how much time it will take, whether you will be able to do it, or if people will think that you are strange, you are focusing on your anxieties. Most of that stuff will not be as bad as you fear it will.

But, what if you focus on the rewards? Do you remember thinking about your birthday when you were a kid? You didn't think about another year going by, or about the new responsibilities you would have. No, you thought about the *presents* you would get from friends and relatives.

Don't focus on fears. It will cost you time.

---

strategies that help them make more while they work less. And they have saved time by patiently living a life within their means.

Both Joe and his wife have friends who are building part-time businesses. They begin to investigate several companies and eventually partner with one that seems to suit their style and ambitions. Their goal is to grow their businesses as quickly as possible. They want to replace her income and create an additional $20,000 per year.

Instead of the anticipated extra year of work, Joe's wife actually had to work another 18 months on her job. But, at the end of that time, they have replaced her salary. She is now free to spend her time raising the kids.

Suddenly, this gives them even more time to devote to their business. Instead of working for another person's dream, Joe's wife is able to devote some extra time to their partners in the business. This makes their time worth even more.

In one more year, they have Joe's income plus an additional $50,000 per year. And Joe is now making more money on his job because *the habit of increasing the value of his time has spread to everything he does.* Not only does his time in his new business become more valuable, the time he spends doing everything becomes more valuable.

Joe and his wife now evaluate their actions. They are always asking themselves, "Will this help us reach our goals? Can I do things differently to be more valuable?" They continue the habits of planning for the future.

Now—and only now—they are ready to move. Now they can afford the new house and the vacation. Even more importantly, they will have the time to enjoy those things. Their kids have gained a full-time mother, and they will grow up with parents who are examples of acting like they are worth more before they start living like they are worth more.

What will Frank's kids get? They will see parents who work for someone else's dream, who are always working to pay something off, trying to fix the past. They inherit the habit of debt.

What Happens When Your Time Changes Value

To help you understand the power of changing the value of your time, consider this situation. Suppose you worked for $25 per hour. One day, your boss says, "I have a great opportunity to offer you. I want you to work 10 hours of overtime each week. I will pay you $500 per hour for the overtime hours."

$500 per hour! You can't believe it. Certainly you will do the extra work. You can make an extra $5,000 per week! You get right on it. You put in your regular 40 hours, and then work the extra 10.

But what happens? After a few weeks, you begin to have some very serious thoughts about the arrangement. You start to think about things that never entered your mind before. Why? Because suddenly you see what really valuable time is. Suddenly, you begin to think about MAXIMIZING the value of that time, not just trading it away.

When you change the value of your time, or when someone changes it for you, you will go through five stages. They are:

Chapter 10 - You _Are_ Worth More

1. *Activity* – *Finish the first 40 hours in two days*

Suppose you are making $25 per hour at your job, a long way from the $500 you get for those 10 hours of overtime. If it were me, I would want to get those first 40 hours over with as soon as possible. I would work 20 hours on Monday, sleep 4 hours and do another 20 hours on Tuesday! After another 4 hours of sleep, I would be there, bright and early, on Wednesday, ready to start earning the big money. A 10 hour shift on Wednesday and I would be finished for the week!

2. *Ambition* – *Can I have some more overtime?*

As long as I am only planning on doing this crazy schedule for a few years, why not see if I can get another 5 hours of $500/hour overtime? After all, I can come in on Thursday, work 5 hours and still have a long weekend every week! Hey boss, can I have 10 more hours of overtime?

3. *Awareness* – *I wonder why I was so poorly paid for the first 40 hours.*

It wouldn't take long for me to realize that the pay for the first 40 hours was much lower than the pay for the overtime. Why was I only getting $25/hour? Ironically, I used to think that $25/hour was the top of my profession! After all, most of my friends only made $20 per hour. Now that $25 seems like a rip off!

4. *Adjustment* – *How does someone act whose time is worth $500 per hour?*

Pretty soon, I start to think, and act, like someone who is worth $500/hour. This will mean a huge change in my attitude and habits. In fact, it might change my whole outlook! If I am going to make some decisions about my time, they will be made more thoughtfully. I can't afford to waste my time, or give it away too cheaply. I need that time to do the big things.

5. *Acceleration* – *Why work the first 40?*

Finally, it hits me. Why should I bother working the first 40 hours? Why not pay someone else to work them, and I will concentrate on the really valuable time? After all, my friends who are making $20 per hour would jump at the chance to make $25. But, wait, I don't want any trouble. I want them to be really motivated. I will pay them $30 per hour. That is a 50% raise! They will be thrilled, right?

Changes in Attitude

It is a matter of certainty! If you start to make some of your time more valuable, it will change your thinking. Your attitude will change and this will lead to even bolder thoughts. Look at the five stages of thinking in the example above.

Notice what happens. When presented with a new opportunity, the first inclination is to increase activity. This increase is a good thing, as long as that activity is well directed. Then, as soon as someone has a little success, they want more! This is the stage where ambition kicks in. It is *so* important to help people achieve even a little success, right from the beginning.

If you are building a business with partners, get them into the activities that will make them successful. Then, do everything possible to get them some success, even a small bit of it, as soon as you possibly can. This will send them on the road to a real life-changing experience.

After a bit of success, it isn't long before you start to realize that what you *are* doing is different and better than what you *were* doing. This is the awareness stage. Sometimes, it can be quite shocking. All of a sudden, you understand just how little you have valued your time! At this stage, many people actually feel regret and remorse for the time that they wasted. They are suddenly painfully aware of the opportunities they lost!

I speak from personal experience here. I didn't start to really improve the value of my time until well into my 40's. I sometimes look back on those years of under-valued time with some real pangs of regret. Where would I be now if I had started to increase the value of my time in my 30's? I don't let it keep me from building high-value time now, but it sure does bother me sometimes!

The end of the awareness stage is a real tipping point. It is at this point that the person on the time-value trail makes a break with past habits. They start to accept their new role and begin to *think* like a person with high value time.

If you can make it into the adjustment stage, you are probably on your way for good. You learn to act like a person with high value time. You surround yourself with other, high value people. Your goals change and your attention to detail grows. You are moving ahead.

Finally, you enter the most exciting stage—acceleration. Only someone who has achieved this level can really appreciate the "stone rolling downhill" effect of increasing the value of their time. It is amazing how quickly you gain momentum and learn to leverage your time into great wealth.

The habits you form to achieve higher value time in part of your life will take over ALL the hours of your life. You will suddenly find yourself surrounded by other people who are on the move. Their interests, their ideas and their ambitions will fuse with yours to form a network of powerful, high value people.

At this point, you will never go back. Even if business fortunes cause a setback, you will never think of yourself as a low value person—ever! *You will have become one of those unique individuals who can always do it again, because you will never allow your time to be undervalued.* You will make the decisions, the friends and the strategies that will always propel you to a time wealthy life.

Give __Yourself__ the Raise

The example above, as exciting as it may be, started because your boss gave you the opportunity to make more money. While this may happen, it is very unlikely! You don't want to wait for someone else to recognize the value of your time.

Yet, we have been trained to ask someone else what we are worth. When we interview for a job, we may tell them what we want, but we have to wait for them to tell us what they are willing to pay. This is a real problem for anyone who wants to increase the value of their time. You see, the only one who can place the correct value on your time is *you.*

There is an old saying about jobs and pay: *On any job, they pay you just enough to keep you from quitting.* If you receive a salary, or even if you work by the hour, your pay is always determined by market conditions, not your true value.

How many companies tell their employees, "You can earn a bonus up to a certain percentage of your salary."? How foolish is that? Yet, it is done all the time. So, if you make $100,000 and your company tells you that you can make up to 25% of your salary in a bonus, then no matter how good you are, you can only earn up to $125,000. That's it. End of story!

Why do companies do this? I honestly can't tell you. There is no good reason for it. It promotes mediocrity and limits the ability of the best people to increase the value of their time. But, that is the way some executives think. And, because they think that way, you have to give *yourself* a raise. You have to be the one to determine what your time is worth. You are the only one who can truly achieve time wealth by raising the value of your time to meet your dreams.

How Do You Give Yourself a Raise?

Folks, here is the plan—the only plan.

First, determine how much you need. Put it in dollar amounts. Do you want a new home, or to bring a spouse home from work for good, or to send your kids to any college they can qualify for? Each of these dreams has a dollar value. Calculate it.

Second, set aside 10 hours per week and build time value within those hours. Do you need an extra $20,000 per year? Then you will need an additional $400 per week, or $40 per hour for those 10 hours. Are you looking for $100,000 per year? You will need $2,000 per week, or $200 per hour for those extra 10 hours.

Third, find a company or system that will meet your goals. If your boss will not give you a raise, give one to yourself by developing your own business on the side. Your business may remain part-time, or it might grow into a full-time endeavor.

Fourth, as your business grows, you will learn to work differently by thinking differently. You will soon become aware that your old way of doing business—trading time for dollars—was never going to allow you to reach the full potential of time value.

Finally, let the new ideas, the new friends and the new practices accelerate your time value. The "10 hours" will soon take over your whole life. Even if you never leave your current source of income, you will find that your time is becoming a much more valuable commodity.

Chapter 11

The Price of Moving On

---

*Price is everything you give up to get
what you want.*

— Philip Kotler

In the last few chapters, we have spoken about how much your time needs to be worth: $100/hour, $200/hour, $500/hour, or more. The real question is, what does your time need to be worth in order for you to live the life you want?

Before you set off on a plan to change the value of your time, you need to have a goal, a target, and a dream. You must know exactly what you need in order to have what you want and deserve.

Your primary goal should be to attain a valuable life. This means several things. First, there should be enough money coming in to support a great lifestyle. Second, you should have the time to enjoy that lifestyle. And finally, a truly valuable life is one that is spent giving value to others. To really enjoy your life, you need to help others enjoy theirs.

Turning S.M.I.L.E.S. Into Dreams

In my best-selling book *10 Rules to Break & 10 Rules to Make: The Do's and Don'ts for Designing Your Destiny*, we use the acronym S.M.I.L.E.S. to describe the stages of dreams and achievement that people seek. Here is a brief summary of those stages:

S — **Survival Dreams.** People want to have as much as it takes to get through the month. They can't dream about a boat if they can't pay the rent.

M —Material Dreams. People want things. That is fine, as long as they can afford them.

I — **Income Dreams.** Some people have dreams of making a certain amount of money. That is great, as long as they learn how to sustain that income without trading away their time.

L — **Lifestyle Dreams.** I sometimes ask people, "What would you do first if you had time and money?" The most popular answer is "Travel." Lifestyle is money *and* the time to spend it.

E — **Expressive Dreams.** How would you express yourself if time and money were not a problem? Would you learn to play music? Would you start a charity?

S — **Spiritual Dreams**. To me, the best way to serve God is to serve your fellow man. Wouldn't it be wonderful to have the time to help others? Wouldn't it be even more wonderful if you could serve people by being a great example?

People move through the dream stages in order. They start out with the lower level stages—survival, material and income—and then move on to the higher levels—lifestyle, expressive and spiritual. It is a natural progression. Learn to ask people where they are now and then show them how to move on.

Where are you in the dream stages? Are you looking for enough money and time to just make it through the month? Or are you at the point where you want to finish off your financial journey by showing others how to finish theirs?

The Price of Moving On

Wherever you are on the dream scale, it will cost you money to move on. Going from the survival phase to the material phase has a price. If you have just been making enough to pay the mortgage, and now you want a new car, there is a price. If you have been making a good income, but your spouse is working as well, reducing your family's lifestyle, there is a price to move on. If you want to have much more leisure, without reducing your income and cash flow, there is a price.

Whatever your dream, quantify its cost. That becomes the goal. That is the amount of money you need to have. Then, determine what your time needs to be worth in order to have that dream!

My wife Jeanne and I faced a decision when we were expecting our first child, and Jeanne was suddenly confined to bed rest. She was making about $55,000 per year. We knew that we wanted her to stay home full time once the baby was born, but her medical condition moved that time frame up by five months. We faced a choice: Reduce our lifestyle or increase my income!

We had no problem determining what the cost of replacing her income was going to be. She was making $55,000. Now, if she stayed at home, we would save some money on work clothes, continuing education, and so forth. So the gap was down to $50,000.

We also knew we didn't want to diminish our lifestyle by my taking a second job. So, we needed to increase the value of my time. We did just that, using the steps I describe in this book.

A few years later, we had a second dream. We wanted to live on the water and have a boat. That cost money. We calculated the cost and that became part of our goal. We reached that goal too.

Recently, we decided that our children should have investments and real estate to start them off in life. So, we are busily working on that. Guess what? It costs money! And again, I didn't want to spend my whole life working, so we had to choose businesses and projects that met our financial criteria.

What about you? Where are you on the dream scale? Where would you like to be? How much will that cost? How much time do you want to spend attaining your dream?

Play With Pain

A few seasons ago, I was watching the Super Bowl on television. One of the quarterbacks was injured, but he continued to play. Eventually his team won the game—the BIGGEST game in football. A reporter interviewed him after the game and asked the usual questions.

Time Out – I Have a Dream

You have to have a dream, a vision, of what you want your life to be. Without a dream, you will not be able to overcome Time Poverty, because you will not be able to overcome challenges. A dream will drive you.

But, a dream has to be specific. You need to have an unquestioned and ceaseless desire to reach specific outcomes.

Here is a great example. A friend of mine told me, "I have a dream. I want to be rich and have lots of time with my family."

This broad statement fails the dream test. It isn't specific enough. How does he define "rich"? Why does he want to be rich? What will he do with the money? How will he spend time with his family?

This man needs to sit down with his wife to come up with specific details about their vision for the future. Then they can come up with a plan to meet their dreams.

"Why did you keep on playing after you were hurt?" asked the reporter.

"Hey, this is the SUPER BOWL," said the quarterback. "I was only going to get one chance to win this thing. I just PLAYED WITH PAIN. I can rest tomorrow."

Folks, that is the story of life. It is the story of perseverance and determination. It is the story for everyone who wants to get off the Fast Track at work. It is going to hurt— for awhile.

This quarterback knew something that you need to know. The pain of playing is not nearly as great as the pain of not playing.

When Jeanne and I decided to move to a lifestyle on the water, we were in pain.

Once we bought into our dream, the pain of not having that dream became overwhelming. (We were depressed whenever we came home from a trip to the beach!) So, we started playing with pain. We knew our lives were out of balance. But, we also knew that if we did nothing, our lives would be out of balance forever. We knew that the lives of our children would be out of balance forever also.

We started working hard—very hard. We had to commit to a long period of *learning* before we started our *earning*.

But, the rewards have been worth it! The rewards are stunning. We live on the water, with our boat at the dock in our backyard. The ocean is just a block away and the Intracoastal Waterway is at our doorstep.

We don't even think about the pain now. It has subsided, and the healthy glow of the rewards is bright in our lifestyle.

Jeanne says it is like childbirth. She tells me that the pain is very intense, but you soon forget about that and the rewards go on for a lifetime. (Men, you better learn to play with pain too. You need your own story!)

Black Holes & Time Bandits

Besides learning to play with pain, you will have to overcome two other types of obstacles that can block you on your journey to time freedom. I call them **Black Holes** and **Time Bandits**.

Black Holes are bad beliefs. We have been taught things that just aren't true, but most of us believe them. **Time Bandits** are disruptive and wasteful people and practices. People can do things that cost you time and money. Practices are things we all do that waste our time.

Black Holes

According to astronomer Carl Sagan, a Black Hole is a spot in space where there is absolutely no light, but there is a star. This star is so heavy that it imploded under the weight of its own gravity. It became smaller and smaller, denser and denser, until it just sort of got sucked into itself!

Here is the really amazing part. The star is still there, even though you can't see it. The pull of gravity is so strong that the light can't escape. And the gravity is so strong that any light from any other star that happens to pass by will also be sucked into this hole in space.

In life, Black Holes are bad beliefs. They are invisible, yet very strong. If you get close to bad beliefs, or associate with people who have bad beliefs, you are in big trouble. You might be a shining star, but the gravitational pull of a Black Hole is so strong it will suck the light right out of you!

Here are some examples of Black Holes:

• I'll wait for things to change

Many people postpone action because they want to wait for things to change. I remember hearing a man say, "Things will be better next year." This man had been doing the same thing for 25 years, without a single change, and he was *still* waiting for things to get better! This is a particularly dangerous, time killing belief because it stops people from taking action.

• More time will solve my problems

No, because the lack of time is *not* your problem. Not knowing how to use that time is the problem. If you do a bad job with the first 24 hours in each day, then what makes you think you would do better with one or two hours more?

• Hard work is its own reward

It is staggering how many people believe this. It is appalling how many bosses believe this. Hard work is not the reward, the *reward* is the reward. You have to learn to believe that. It is important for two reasons:

First, you will never get other people to take action if you think they are happy to do the work for the work itself. Second, you need to structure your own rewards, and then choose the work that brings you those specific rewards.

• Changing jobs will change your fortune

Changing your job will *not* change your fortune—especially if you count your fortune by the amount of time you have! If you are trading your time for dollars, then it doesn't matter who you trade it with. You will never reach your time goals. You will only change your business cards.

• Stress is natural

Stress is *not* a natural byproduct of making a living. You are stressed out because you do not have enough time and money. You are stressed out because the system you chose to follow is robbing you of your life.

It is no wonder you think that stress is natural. Everyone around you is stressed out as well. But it doesn't have to be that way.

- ## Results are all that matter

Yes, results are great—if they are the right results. However, so many people are looking for the wrong results to begin with.

If you focus only on results, you will miss so much of the beauty of life. You will overlook the possibility that you can enjoy yourself while you are on the way to the results.

Time Bandits

Time Bandits, just like any other bandit, rob you of your valuables. Of course, the "valuables" in this case are your precious hours of time. Time bandits are practices we have, like not being able to say "no", or having an open-door policy at work. Clutter is another Time Bandit.

And don't forget the people who consistently waste your time! You know who they are.

Why not make a "Most Wanted" list of all the Time Bandits in your life? Then put them away, for a life sentence.

Giving Up Old Habits—How Great a Cost?

It is hard to let go! You have lived with your beliefs and practices for a very long time. One of the costs of moving on is the pain of letting go, the pain of changing.

The price you pay to give up your old habits will depend entirely on the strength of your dreams. Folks, in my speeches and presentations, I always tell my audiences the secret for changing their lives. I will share it with you here:

If you want to change your life, then you have to change your life!

I can't tell you what the cost of moving on will be for you. I can only tell you that you *have* to pay it in order to move on.

Get over those bad beliefs, give up those bad practices and stay away from the people who are Time Bandits. The price is worth it. Make some changes, and buy back your "S.M.I.L.E.S."

Chapter 12

Winning the Time Game

---

*Don't say you don't have enough time.
You have exactly the same number of
hours per day that were given to Helen
Keller, Pasteur, Michelangelo, Mother
Theresa, Leonardo da Vinci, Thomas
Jefferson, and Albert Einstein.*

— H. Jackson Brown

Bad, Better, Best!

By now, I hope you realize that most of your time problems do
not come from over scheduling, or a lack of efficiency, or the pres-
sures of society. If you are like the vast majority of us, your time
problems come from one source—trading your time on a one-to-
one basis for one-to-one results.

In order to really change your life, you have to change the way
you think about time. You need to change the way you get
results.

In this chapter, we will look at three ways that people have
used to create a more time-wealthy lifestyle. I will expose you to
a "bad" technique (the one most people use), then show you a better technique (it will work but cost you time), and finally we'll
look at the best technique I know for overcoming Time Poverty—
achieving more and working less.

Method 1—The Bad Way: "I need more money, so I'll work more hours."

"Our lives are so busy," a friend recently told me. "We both work full time. It seems like we are always running, trying to catch up with things. But our kids start college in two years and we don't have enough money set aside for them. I'm thinking about taking another job to make some extra money."

Have you heard something like this before? It always amazes me. People are worried about having enough time, but they are also worried about having enough money to do the things they want. How do they solve their problems? They work overtime or take a second job! How does that make sense?

Far too many Americans are caught in a vicious trap. They work hard, harder than almost anyone else in the world, but they still don't have enough money to do the things they want. And because they work so many hours, they don't have the time they need. But, they try to solve both problems by doing the same thing that got them into trouble in the first place.

For many people, overtime or a second

Time Out – More Work, Less Money

Serena is a Dental Surgery Assistant. She works at a thriving practice with three doctors. She makes about $45,000 per year for a 45-hour work week. Her time on her job is worth $20 per hour.

Serena wants to purchase a house. She needs extra money for both the down-payment and the monthly mortgage payments.

Since no overtime was available at her job, she solved her money problem by working each weekend at a local discount store as a cashier. She puts in an eight hour shift every Saturday and Sunday. However, her second job pays a lot less than her primary source of income. She makes about $12 per hour at the discount store. After taxes, she is able to take home about $140 each week.

What if Serena did something different? Instead of working at a low paying job each weekend, what if she invested the same amount of time into a business of her own? She could then leverage her time, instead of trading it for dollars. Serena needs to change her thinking and actions in order to change her life.

---

job is a "temporary" thing. For example, they need a new car, so they work nights and weekends until they have enough for a down payment on that car. Notice that I said "down payment". I didn't say they worked long enough to pay for the new car entirely. No, they work just long enough to get themselves into another payment! Then, they can't stop working that second job. They MUST put in the extra hours because they have now incurred more debt.

Do you understand why working a second job or working more hours on your present job is a bad idea? Even if you solve some short-term money problems, spending more time at work will CERTAINLY NOT solve your time problems!

If you are caught in the work and spend cycle, then you have to change the fundamental way you look at time and money. Don't trade the work and spend cycle for the work more and spend more cycle!

Method 2—A Better Way: "Make more, then invest it!"

There is a better way. It is not a great way, but it's better than the work and spend cycle you are probably in now. It is the work-and-invest cycle.

Earlier in this book, you learned about the importance of establishing income-producing equities that allow you to keep more of your time, while giving you the income to secure your financial needs. You can do this by working more hours, then investing the money to create future income from your assets.

Let me give you an example. At age 35, Caroline realized that she would have to do something different, or she would never have the money to send her kids to college. As a professional nurse, she made a decent living. Combined with her husband Justin's salary, they had enough money to make the payments on their two cars, their four-bedroom home and to take a one-week vacation each year. Caroline and her husband did not spend more than they made. In fact, they were able to save a little bit each year, but not enough for college tuition for the children.

The hospital where Caroline worked was always asking her to work overtime. She didn't like it. The kids were growing so fast, and her husband worked extra hours too. She didn't want to be an "absentee mom", but she also didn't want to go into debt.

Caroline made a decision—and a plan. She would work two extra hours per day, and one extra shift on the weekends. She earned $25 per hour for each of the extra 18 hours per week, or about an extra $22,000 per year. The couple's first thought when the money started rolling in? "Maybe we should get a new SUV!" But, they stuck to their dream of paying for their two children's education.

They estimated that by the time the children went to college, each child would need between $70,000 and $90,000 for 4 years of tuition, books, fees, and room & board. If Caroline earned an extra $22,000 per year, minus taxes, it could take over a decade to "save" the money. She would miss so much time with her kids!

The couple came up with a better plan—one that would give them the money they needed, but that would also give them a life together. Here is what they did:

Caroline decided she was willing to give up her spare time for five years to create the college fund. Her husband agreed to take over some of the household duties, especially making dinner and getting the girls ready for bed. When Caroline got home each night, the whole family ate together, and then spent a half-hour reading.

Instead of putting the extra money into a bank account, the couple used the funds to purchase some rental homes. At the end of year one, they bought a house for $100,000 and rented it out. The rent paid the mortgage, and Justin took over the responsibilities of maintaining the rental property, collecting the rent and paying the bills. At the end of year two, they bought another house. They then used equity from the first house for the down payment on a third home.

At the end of four years, one year early, Caroline was able to give up the extra weekend shift. Six months later, she cut back on her hours at work to completely get rid of the overtime. Today, the houses are doing fine and the tenants are "paying" for the mortgages. In a few years, when the kids go to college, Justin and Caroline can sell some of the houses, or take out a second mortgage on the increased equity. The proceeds will pay for the kids' college tuitions.

What is the lesson here? By giving up some time now, Caroline and Justin were able to GAIN time later on. Instead of giving in to their first impulse and buying a new car, they invested their extra money into income-producing assets. By creating a plan to fill their dreams, and by investing rather than spending, Caroline and Justin created a life, and a life lesson. They can teach their kids to do the same thing and make their family's fortune better for generations.

Method 3—The Best Way: "Leverage your time, lessen your Time Poverty—permanently!"

Caroline and Justin were on the right track. They had learned to turn their dreams into a plan, and their plans into reality. They understood that the earn-and-spend cycle would never give them what they really wanted. But they didn't *maximize* their work. They made several mistakes that cost them both time and money.

Folks, working extra shifts and putting the money into income-producing assets is certainly better than working extra hours and spending that money on debt producing liabilities. However, Caroline and Justin's system is only the better way, not the best way to gain control over your time and wealth.

In fact, there are two problems with Caroline and Justin's methods. First, no matter how hard she worked, Caroline could only make $25 per hour at her job. So every time she needed an extra $25, she had to work an extra hour. That is all the hospital would pay for the overtime. Second, when she stopped working the extra hours, the extra money stopped coming in! After four years of working an extra 18 hours per week, Caroline was exhausted. She couldn't do that for a lifetime. And, even if she did, it would solve her money problems, but not her time problems.

Let's look at an alternative plan for Justin and Caroline and see how they can leverage their time and dollars. And, more importantly, let's see how they can create income that continues for a lifetime.

Caroline and Justin are both 35, with two small kids and a dream: They want to pay for their kids' college educations. They happened to mention this dream to one of their friends. "We just don't know how to do it," says Caroline. "We are thinking about working extra hours for a while to raise some investment money."

"If you are serious about making that extra money for your kids' college tuitions, I can introduce you to some business owners who can help you reach your goals," said the friend. And, he did.

Caroline and Justin were skeptical at first. After all, why would strangers help them? Why would someone else give up his time to help them reach their goals? It just didn't seem to make sense.

The couple went to a seminar and learned how to leverage their time. They discovered the best way to reach their time and money goals. They became independent business owners and created a network of other business owners. Here's how it worked.

Instead of working extra hours on a job, Caroline and Justin put those hours into their personal business. Their sponsors, the people who helped them start their business, were willing to help Justin and Caroline because the sponsors made money whenever Justin and Caroline made money.

The couple learned a lot about business. Their company sold consumable products—things that people use again and again. So, when they created customers for their products, those customers reordered. (Customer Equity). Justin and Caroline also made money when they helped other people start a business and make money (Network Equity). And, as they became more established, they were able to make even more money by helping still more people (Mentor Equity).

The couple still invested the money they made into rental properties. And, those properties appreciated in value as the renters paid the mortgage. The couple is definitely on track to pay for their kids' education. But there are several *major* differences between Method 2 (A Better Way) and Method 3 (The BEST Way).

Here are a few of the differences:

- Instead of working an additional 18 hours per week when her BOSS wanted her to work, Caroline did the extra work when it was convenient for her. And, Justin was able to work on the business too, DOUBLING their efforts.

- Instead of limiting the value of their time to $25 per hour, they could make their time worth WHATEVER they wanted.
- After four years, they weren't exhausted, they were excited!
- Instead of cutting out the extra 18 hours per week after four years of hard work, Caroline was able to cut her JOB back to 18 hours per week.
- The couple made a lot of new friends and helped many people reach their dreams.
- Eventually, the couple can stop working, and their business will continue to grow and produce income.

They now have the opportunity to have a lifelong income, *and* the time to enjoy it!

The BEST Way to Overcome Time Poverty

If you really want to break out of the mold, if you really want to make a life, not just a living, then you have to follow some simple rules. There is absolutely no way around it.

You must leverage your time. Working more hours may solve your money problems, but it will not solve your time problems. You must *invest* your extra money into income-producing assets. Otherwise, you will simply be caught in the work and spend cycle that has ruled your life to this point.

You must have a business of your own—one that allows you to utilize the time of others. And you must have a dream that drives you through all the tough times. Without a dream, without a reason for doing things differently, you will fall victim to the very first excuse or obstacle that you face. But a specific dream, coupled with the appropriate plan and action, will allow you to truly overcome Time Poverty. You will have the money—and the time—for a fantastic lifestyle.

Chapter 13

A Time-Rich Life

---

*A year from now you will wish you
had started today.*

— Karen Lamb

If you want to overcome Time Poverty, follow these five steps:

1. **Get a dream**
2. **Give your job a break and get off the Fast Track**
3. **Create a personal business**
4. **Create income-producing equity**
5. **Retire on Mentor Equity**

It is Time to Get Started

Okay, your life is a mess. The kids are overscheduled, you and your spouse are working too much, the dog needs to go to the veterinarian, and you don't have time to make major changes in your life right now. Fine. Make some small changes in your actions, but some major changes in your beliefs and attitudes.

Here is a thought for anyone who is bogged down with the challenge of completely changing their life. There is one thing you can change that doesn't take any time at all. Change your mind! I know you have the time to do that!

But the Task is Overwhelming!

Question: How do you eat an elephant?

Answer: One bite at a time!

If you are still feeling overwhelmed by the challenge of overcoming Time Poverty, don't worry about it. You are not alone. You're probably thinking, "I am so far from where I want to be that I can never do all the things necessary to reach my goals."

Well, if you keep thinking like that, you never will! You can't look at the whole problem all at once. You have to break it down into reasonable steps. If you don't take some small steps, you will never have the time you want.

Listen to the Experts

I once attended a seminar for independent business owners. We had a real treat during the second day. The master motivator, Zig Ziglar, was scheduled to speak. Everyone was ready, excited and eager. This man had the answers!

During his talk, Mr. Ziglar asked us all a question. "Would you like to have one more hour each day to get things done?" I can tell you that every single person in that audience was ready to hear this!

"Just get up an hour earlier each day and get started," he said.

I was stunned. This was the answer? This is what the EXPERT had to say? I could have figured that out myself! Sure, if I got up an hour earlier and got going, I would have an extra hour per day. But I mean, come on, couldn't Zig Ziglar do better than that?

It took me many years folks, but I finally figured it out. The answer is "NO." Zig Ziglar, or any expert for that matter, could not do better for me than by saying, "Get up an hour earlier and get started." It didn't matter how much I learned at the seminar. It didn't matter how many motivating speeches I heard. It didn't matter what anyone else told me. Until I decided to change my mind and take the first step, I would never take *any* steps.

Find the time somewhere. Get up an hour earlier, or turn off the television, or skip the newspaper for one night. If you think about it too much, you will never do it.

In a recent sermon, our pastor David Rees said, "It is easier to act your way into thinking than to think your way into acting." His message was simple. You can do it if you just do it!

Let Go—and GROW!

So, here we are, almost at the end of this book. It is time to make the decisions and take the actions that will change your life. Stop worrying. You are not the first one to face this challenge. A whole lot of people, me included, have already done what you are about to do. How did we do it? We just started!

When Jeanne and I made our decision to change our lives—on July 7, 1993, at 2:30 in the afternoon, we were overwhelmed by the task that lay before us. But, we made a simple decision. We set a workable goal that we still follow to this day. Here is what we decided:

Are You A Winner or A Whiner?

It takes less time to be a winner than a whiner. A whiner is someone who complains about his or her "luck." A whiner is always comparing themselves to others. A whiner takes up a lot of time and energy complaining about how unfair things are. Did you ever notice that a whiner repeats themselves a lot? They tell the same sad story again and again.

Winners, on the other hand, don't waste time. Winners are always talking about the present and the future, not the past. Winners are positive people who don't have time for worrying, complaining or comparing. They want to move ahead in life.

Winners are willing to make any change necessary in order to succeed. They don't make the same mistakes again and again. They meet challenges head on and overcome them.

Decide to be a winner, not a whiner. It will save you a lot of time.

We would not let the sun set on a day when we did not take one step forward.

That isn't so bad, is it? We knew we couldn't solve the entire problem on any one day, but we also knew that every day was a gift to be used. We decided to just do something each day. It might be a few minutes of reading a positive book, or, in my case, writing a positive book. It might be a home strategy meeting to assess our goals. It could be writing some e-mails, making some phone calls or any number of things. But, each day since July 7, 1993, we have tried to do something positive—something that turns us from whiners to winners, from the time-broke to the Time-Rich!

It is Time for a Timetable

Let's look at each of the five steps for overcoming Time Poverty and establish a timetable for success. How long will it take you to become time-wealthy? It depends entirely on you. After Jeanne and I made the decision, it took us about 5 years to really reach our goals. But, we had a lot of smaller successes along the way. Those smaller successes kept us going.

Here are a few suggestions for you. Remember, everyone is different. Don't compare yourself to others.

STEP 1 – Develop a dream—a vision for your life

You should be able to do this within a week. Be specific, and be honest. What do you really want? What is really important to you? Don't forget to prioritize.

Our big dream was to live on the water. We described the kind of home we wanted, where it should be and how big a dock space we needed. We also described the type of boat we wanted, how many vacations we would take per year, what kind of schools we would send our daughters to, and how often we wanted to travel to visit our parents. In other words, we described in detail what we wanted for ourselves and the people we loved.

But, Jeanne and I did something that not everyone does. We estimated how much this lifestyle would COST! I wanted to know what I needed to make in order to enjoy the things we wanted. Then, I simply looked for opportunities that helped me achieve that income—without working so hard that I didn't have the time to enjoy it.

Checklist for your dream – Consider the following:

1. Your Home
   a. Where do you want to live?
   b. What kind of home do you want?
   c. How big should it be?
   d. Do you want any special amenities, like entertainment facilities?

2. Vacations
   a. Where will you go?
   b. How often?
   c. How will you travel?

3. Family
   a. Parents—Do they have a nice home?
   b. Siblings—Do they need help?
   c. Children—Where will they go to school? Where will they live?

4. Retirement
   A. When?
   B. What will you do?

Put timelines and cost estimates on every item.

STEP 2—Give your job a break and get off the Fast Track at work

I already had a job I loved — being a college professor. But I was getting some offers to "move up the ladder" into administration. In fact, my name was placed into nomination to become the Dean of a very prestigious school.

However, I made the decision that being a professor would be my LAST job. Becoming a Dean or a University Vice-President would have given me a raise in both salary and prestige, but not what I really wanted—time and money freedom. Not only did I decide to remain a professor, I also decided to teach less! A few years ago, I stopped teaching summer school. I no longer needed the money. In a few more years, I plan to stop teaching entirely.

How about you? Are you ready for Step 2? You may not have the time or the money to switch to a job you really love. However, you can make an immediate decision to get off the Fast Track. Do your job well. Become so good at it that you are seen as the best, most valuable employee in that position. But, look for solutions to your time problems outside your job.

Starting today, decide that you will look to yourself for a raise. Decide that your family's wealth depends upon what you do in your spare time, not on your work time.

Checklist for your job:

1. What would be the perfect job for you?

2. What hours would you like to work?

3. What do you like about your current job?

4. Could you work less hours at your present job? If so, what would it take?

5. What could you do better at your job to make it more secure?

6. What could you do to be the best at your current position?

7. Are you satisfied to stay in this position? If not, what could you do to make this position better?

STEP 3—Develop a personal business that leverages the value of your time

Okay, you have an estimate of how much your dream is going to cost. You have made the decision that the money is NOT going to come from your job. Now, it is time to find a personal business that WILL pay for your dream.

How long should it take you to identify the right business opportunity? I don't think it should take more than 60—90 days. There are so many opportunities out there. And, the cost of entry for most of them is so low that you don't need to make a huge investment to get started.

What makes a good personal business? Think about what you are trying to achieve. You want to make money, of course, but you also want to create equity. The money will enable you to buy some things, but the equity will set you free. So, look at the EQUITY-GENERATING potential of your personal business.

The equity in your business will allow you to leverage the value of your time. Leverage is what you are looking for! On your job, you get an hour's pay for every hour of work. When you leverage, you still do an hour of work, but you get more than an hour's worth of pay for it. And, more importantly, when you create the right kind of equity, you can get paid even when you are no longer working!

The right personal business can generate three kinds of equity: Customer, System and Network Equity. (See Chapter 7, *The Ecstasy of Equity*.) Each of these equities can leverage the value of your time.

Checklist for your Personal Business:

Look for a business with the following opportunities:

1. Consumable products

2. Good reputation for quality and warranties

3. Standardized ordering, delivery and payment systems

4. Training

5. Successful people

6. No-limit rewards

7. Sponsorship programs

8. Low entry costs

9. High ethical standards

STEP 4—Invest in equities and assets

It is easy to make money in a personal business. It is harder to turn that money into long-term, income-producing assets and equities. It requires discipline.

When most people first start making extra money, they spend that money on "stuff." That is fine at first. You need to treat yourself to some nice things. It is motivating and will keep you going. However, no amount of stuff will give you time. Only residual income from leveraged equities will give you time.

What you need to do is trade your time for income-producing equities. Let those *equities* produce the money, while you spend your time on other things. That is the ONLY way to overcome Time Poverty.

What kind of equities should you generate? Well, we have already seen how a personal business can produce Customer, System and Network equities. However, to be really successful, you want to diversify your equities. You want to invest in assets like stock and real estate that are not part of your business. You won't do this right away, but you should have it in your plans.

How long should it take to build these equities? These are long-term strategies. However, you can start right away, even before you have extra income from your personal business. Learn about stocks, bonds and mutual funds. Watch the local real estate market. Read the paper.

Checklist for assets and equities:

1. Stocks, Bonds and Mutual Funds
   a. Do you have an investment account?
   b. Do you have a broker?
   c. What do you know about the stock market?
   d. How have your stocks, bonds and mutual funds been performing?
   e. At this rate, will you have enough to meet your goals?
   f. How much more do you need to invest, and how often do you need to invest it?
2. Real Estate
   a. Where would you like to invest?
   b. Do you know how to buy and sell real estate?
   c. Do you have a relationship with an agent or broker?
   d. What is the average price of the types of property you want?
   e. What are the average rents?
   f. How much can you borrow, and at what costs?
   g. Do you need to hire someone to manage your properties?

STEP 5—Retire on Mentor Equity

Mentor Equity may be the single most important concept for living a fruitful, happy and powerful life. It places value on the experience you have acquired over your lifetime.

During your struggle to overcome Time Poverty, you are going to find people who help you. These people are *your* mentors. They will give of their knowledge, friendship and wisdom. If you are in the right kind of business, these people will profit financially from the help they give you. You, in turn, have an obligation and an opportunity to become a mentor to others.

How do you build Mentor Equity? There is only one way. You must succeed. You must develop experience that can benefit others. And, you must be willing to pass that experience along.

This experience has a great deal of value. When you have acquired it, when you have proven yourself, you will be able to "sell" that Mentor Equity. People will pay to learn what you know. Your life will be rich and full because your opinions and experience will be sought by others. At retirement, whatever age that is, you will not fade into obscurity, you will flourish!

There is no checklist for Mentor Equity, because it is so personal. You will know it when you have it. People will seek you out, ask for your advice, and try to emulate your actions. They will want what you have, and the best ones will be willing to do what you did to get it. Your rewards should be both spiritual and financial. You'll have the satisfaction that comes from helping another person succeed, and, if you package it right, you can achieve the same kind of cash flow from Mentor Equity that comes from other equities.

You Can Do It!

If you have done the right things—set your dream, escaped from the Fast Track, established income-producing equities and a personal business, and are willing to share your experience with others, you can have it all! You can have money, time, and a valuable network of loving, caring and positive people. I don't know how you classify a time-wealthy life, but this sounds pretty good to me!

Your journey from a time-broke, worried and underpaid average person, to a stress free, Time-Rich mentor is just ahead of you. All it takes is the first step, then another, then another.

You are on your way to overcoming Time Poverty!

Time Out – Your Story

Throughout this book, I have stated one fact over and over: You can't overcome Time Poverty by trading your time for dollars. You need to trade your time for EQUITY, and let your equity create dollars. And, I have given you examples of people who remain Time-Poor and those who became Time-Rich.

Now, it is time to tell your story.

Write your success story. In other words, write a story that describes your life in detail—AFTER you achieve time and money freedom. Then, tell yourself how you got there. How long did it take? What were the specific things you had to do? Who helped you?

Finally, end your story with a series of messages, or lessons, you want to pass on. What would you tell your children or your best friends about what you learned? What advice would you give them?

Now, make your story come true.

Remember, the choices you make determine the life that you lead—it's up to you!